**Conversations with
Sarah Schulman**

Literary Conversations Series
Monika Gehlawat
General Editor

Conversations with Sarah Schulman

Edited by Will Brantley

University Press of Mississippi / Jackson

The University Press of Mississippi is the scholarly publishing agency of
the Mississippi Institutions of Higher Learning: Alcorn State University,
Delta State University, Jackson State University, Mississippi State University,
Mississippi University for Women, Mississippi Valley State University,
University of Mississippi, and University of Southern Mississippi.

www.upress.state.ms.us

The University Press of Mississippi is a member
of the Association of University Presses.

Any discriminatory or derogatory language or hate speech regarding race, ethnicity, religion,
sex, gender, class, national origin, age, or disability that has been retained or appears in elided
form is in no way an endorsement of the use of such language outside a scholarly context.

Copyright © 2024 by University Press of Mississippi
All rights reserved
Manufactured in the United States of America
∞

Library of Congress Cataloging-in-Publication Data

Names: Brantley, Will (William Oliver), editor.
Title: Conversations with Sarah Schulman / Will Brantley.
Other titles: Literary conversations series.
Description: Jackson : University Press of Mississippi, 2024. | Series: Literary
  conversations series | Includes bibliographical references and index.
Identifiers: LCCN 2023033385 (print) | LCCN 2023033386 (ebook) |
  ISBN 9781496848314 (hardback) | ISBN 9781496848321 (trade paperback) |
  ISBN 9781496848338 (epub) | ISBN 9781496848345 (epub) |
  ISBN 9781496848352 (pdf) | ISBN 9781496848369 (pdf)
Subjects: LCSH: Schulman, Sarah, 1958—Interviews. | Authors, American—United
  States—Interviews. | Women authors, American—Interviews. | Women dramatists,
  American—Interviews. | Gay activists—United States—Interviews.
Classification: LCC PS3569.C5393 Z46 2024 (print) | LCC PS3569.C5393 (ebook) |
  DDC 818/.5409—dc23/eng/20231115
LC record available at https://lccn.loc.gov/2023033385
LC ebook record available at https://lccn.loc.gov/2023033386

British Library Cataloging-in-Publication Data available

Books by Sarah Schulman

The Sophie Horowitz Story. Tallahassee: Naiad Press, 1984.
Girls, Visions and Everything. Seattle: Seal Press, 1986.
After Delores. New York: Dutton, 1988.
People in Trouble. New York: Dutton, 1990.
Empathy. New York: Dutton, 1992.
My American History: Lesbian and Gay Life during the Reagan/Bush Years. New York: Routledge, 1994; Second Edition, 2019.
Rat Bohemia. New York: Dutton, 1995.
Collected Early Novels of Sarah Schulman: The Sophie Horowitz Story; Girls, Visions and Everything; After Delores. New York: Quality Paperback Book Club, 1997.
Shimmer. New York: Avon, 1998.
Stagestruck: Theater, AIDS, and the Marketing of Gay America. Durham: Duke University Press, 1998.
Carson McCullers (Historically Inaccurate). New York: Playscripts, 2006.
The Child. New York: Carroll and Graf, 2007.
Mercy. New York: Belladonna Books, 2008.
The Mere Future. Vancouver: Arsenal Pulp Press, 2009.
Ties That Bind: Familial Homophobia and Its Consequences. New York: New Press, 2009.
The Gentrification of the Mind: Witness to a Lost Imagination. Berkeley: University of California Press, 2012.
Israel/Palestine and the Queer International. Durham: Duke University Press, 2012.
The Cosmopolitans. New York: Feminist Press at CUNY, 2016.
Conflict Is Not Abuse: Overstating Harm, Community Responsibility, and the Duty of Repair. Vancouver: Arsenal Pulp Press, 2016.
Maggie Terry. New York: Feminist Press at CUNY, 2018.
Let the Record Show: A Political History of ACT UP, New York, 1987–1993. New York: Farrar, 2021.

Contents

Introduction   xi

Chronology   xv

New Faces   3
   Karla Jay / 1988

A Conversation with Sarah Schulman   6
   Christi Cassidy / 1989

Sarah Schulman   11
   Milyoung Cho / 1993

Sarah Schulman: "I'm There Because I Have Certain Beliefs"   17
   Kate Brandt / 1993

Schulman vs. *Rent*   23
   Achy Obejas / 1997

Man in the Hot Seat   29
   Sarah Schulman and Andrew Sullivan / 1999

Behind *Enemies*' Lines   36
   Dan Bacalzo / 2007

Sarah Schulman's *The Child*: The Toxic Machine   40
   Ernest Hardy / 2007

Monday Interview: Sarah Schulman   44
   Dick Donahue / 2009

An Interview with Sarah Schulman   47
   Carlos Motta / 2011

Interview with Writer Sarah Schulman   62
   Marissa Bell Toffoli / 2011

An Interview with Sarah Schulman   68
   Zoe Whittall / 2013

Writer and Activist Sarah Schulman on *The Normal Heart*, Being Friends with Larry Kramer, and the Whitewashing of AIDS History   79
   E. Alex Jung / 2014

Book Brahmin: Sarah Schulman   84
   Shelf Awareness / 2016

Sarah Schulman on Her Latest Provocations   87
   Chris Freeman / 2016

Close Encounters: Sarah Schulman with Jarrett Earnest   97
   Jarrett Earnest / 2016

The PEN Ten with Sarah Schulman   107
   PEN America / 2017

How to Deal with Conflicts about Ex-Lovers, HIV, Trump, and More   109
   Trenton Straube / 2018

The Inadvertent Postmodernist: A Conversation with Sarah Schulman   117
   Alex Dueben / 2018

Taking Responsibility: An Interview with Sarah Schulman   124
   Carley Moore / 2018

What ACT UP Can Teach Us about the Current Health Emergency: An Interview with Sarah Schulman   131
   Elisa R. Linn / 2020

Good Conflict   135
　Molly Fischer / 2020

Sarah Schulman Discusses Her Massive ACT UP Tome
Let the Record Show, Coming This May   148
　Tim Murphy / 2021

Choral History   157
　Jay Vithalani / 2021

Index   165

Introduction

The word *witness* appears frequently in commentary on Sarah Schulman, a writer who has borne witness to her time and who has taken readers to places where they might not otherwise go. In a promotional blurb for *Stagestruck: Theater, AIDS, and the Marketing of Gay America* (1988), Schulman's book on the commodification of gay culture, historian Martin Duberman praised his friend and fellow writer for remaining what she has always been: "a rare, fearless teller of unpleasant truths."

A witness and a truth teller, Sarah Schulman is also a valued provocateur, one who finds it difficult to celebrate gay marriage when the nation still lacks strong antidiscrimination laws, or to ignore the disparity between the national mourning for 9/11 victims and the absence of such grief for the far greater number of citizens who have died from AIDS. Readers rely on Schulman to challenge their thinking. When she was awarded the 2018 Bill Whitehead Award for Lifetime Achievement from the Publishing Triangle (only one of many honors, all of which are included in the following chronology), Schulman remarked that she has written for the people that she writes about—a community that continues to find itself under siege. This appreciative audience has made Schulman a well-known media presence and will no doubt welcome this volume of interviews that collectively mark major moments of her career.

When Nancy McGuire Roche and I coedited *Conversations with Edmund White* (2017), it occurred to me that Schulman was the obvious choice for my next project. I knew her through our shared attachment to the work of writer Carson McCullers, but I also knew her depictions of New York City's once-gritty East Village—its gay enclaves, the horrors of its AIDS crisis, the pernicious changes brought to it by gentrification. A Jewish lesbian who successfully fuses artistry with social commentary, Schulman is also a true woman of letters, and her oeuvre is extensive. And like Edmund White, she is a terrific conversationalist with a wide array of interviews to draw from.

Schulman's eleven novels (as of this writing) encompass the genres of social realist, historical, speculative, experimental, and lesbian crime fiction—a detective subgenre that Schulman helped to pioneer. Interviews have given Schulman the opportunity to talk about the sources of her fiction and to reflect on her status as a "niche" writer who continually reckons with publishers' fright at lesbian content. While fiction is her primary love, many readers have come to Schulman through her nonfiction (seven books as of this writing). An intriguing example is Barrak Alzaid, a Kuwaiti writer who cites Schulman's *Ties That Bind: Familial Homophobia and Its Consequences* (2009) as the book that saved his life.[1] Through nonfiction Schulman has shaped debates on urban displacement, gay assimilation, human rights in Palestine, and other politically charged topics.

Interviewers often look for connections between the different components of Schulman's career, for she is also a playwright, a filmmaker, a teacher, and a prominent gay rights activist. With filmmaker Jim Hubbard, she coproduced the feature documentary *United in Anger: A History of ACT UP* (2012). With Hubbard she also created an indispensable oral history project devoted to AIDS activism. While each of this project's 187 interviews focuses on a participant in one of the many functions of ACT UP (the AIDS Coalition to Unleash Power), Schulman is a forceful presence in the conversations that she conducted. I encourage readers to browse this vast archive, readily available at actuporalhistory.org.

At their best, interviews provide a blend of autobiography, biography, and cultural history. Interviews prompt personal revelations that become signposts in the critical discourse on a writer. This volume contains many such signposts, starting with a series of interviews as Schulman was establishing herself as a writer of note. These include pieces in the *Village Voice*, the short-lived *Visibilities: A Lesbian Magazine*, *BOMB*, and *Happy Endings: Lesbian Writers Talk about Their Life and Work*, a collection of interviews from Naiad Press, the publisher that launched Schulman's first novel, *The Sophie Horowitz Story* (1984). Speaking with Christie Cassidy at *Visibilities*, Schulman clarified what she found to be "the tricky dichotomy" for a gay writer—the need to present "a person who, on the one hand, is human and flawed, and on the other hand has found a degree of individual strength that many other people in the world lack. That's the challenge."

These pieces are followed by a 1997 *Chicago Tribune* interview with Cuban writer Achy Obejas, who summarizes the controversy surrounding Schulman's novel *People in Trouble* (1990) and its affinity, unacknowledged at the time, with Jonathan Larson's hit Broadway musical, *Rent* (1994). By the late 1990s, Schulman had become well known in LGBT circles and was often called upon to comment on issues related to the culture wars of that

INTRODUCTION xiii

era. It is fun to see her spar in 1999 with conservative gay columnist Andrew Sullivan in the pages of *The Advocate*.

Although her work as a playwright is less known than her fiction and nonfiction, Schulman's drama has been staged at Playwrights Horizons and other cutting-edge venues. Included here is a *TheaterMania* interview on Schulman's adaptation of Isaac Bashevis Singer's *Enemies, A Love Story*, staged in 2007 at Philadelphia's Wilma Theater. Schulman explains why she was drawn to Singer despite their differences: "As an intellectual, I have had to learn that I can't just cut out the greatest works of Western civilization because they're so prejudiced." Schulman takes what she needs from the Western canon and extends it to her own experience and that of her community.

Interviews are most often prompted by the publication of a new work. With *LA Weekly*, Schulman discusses her nearly lost novel, *The Child* (2007); with *Publishers Weekly*, she expands on themes in *Ties That Bind: Familial Homophobia and Its Consequences* (2009); with the literary blog *Words with Writers*, she reflects on the sources that led to her dystopian novel *The Mere Future* (2011); and with the *Los Angeles Review of Books*, she focuses on her return to detective fiction in the novel *Maggie Terry* (2018).

With both the *Brooklyn Rail* and *POZ*, Schulman talks about writing *Conflict Is Not Abuse: Overstating Harm, Community Responsibility, and the Duty of Repair* (2016), a hybrid work of self-reflection and self-help that, in the words of Ezra Klein, "has become a kind of cult classic."[2] Included also are two of the many interviews prompted by the publication of *Let the Record Show: A Political History of ACT UP, New York, 1987–1993* (2021), a book that evolved from Schulman's oral history project. Speaking with *TheBody*, Schulman explains why she chose to conclude her history in 1993: "I didn't want to end it with the 'happy ending' of protease inhibitors arriving in 1996.... I wanted to show how crazy and desperate everyone was at that point, organizing political funerals and riding around in vans with the bodies of their dead friends. I wanted to convey what the suffering was like at that point." Speaking with *A&U*, Schulman defends her belief that oral history does in fact produce revealing patterns when the pool of participants is as large as the one that furnished her record of this great social movement.

Four of the shorter interviews center not on Schulman's work but on topics, including her account to *Vulture* of her friendship with writer and activist Larry Kramer, and her summary to PEN America of the various arrests that have accompanied her activism. With the e-newsletter *Shelf Awareness*, Schulman lists books and authors that have inspired her, and with the art magazine *Frieze*, she comments on differences between the public's response to AIDS and the more recent COVID pandemic. The remaining interviews are notable for inviting Schulman to reflect on the trajectory of her career within the context of LGBT history and culture. These include pieces by Carlos Motta in *We Who Feel Differently*, Zoe Whittall in *The Believer*, Chris Freeman in the *Gay & Lesbian Review Worldwide*, Alex Dueben in *The Rumpus*, and Molly Fischer in *The Cut*. These five interviews range wide and contain some of Schulman's most illuminating comments about her focus and commitments as an artist, teacher, historian, and activist. "I'm realizing," she tells Chris Freeman, "that my theme for my entire body of work is 'why are people mean?'"

A longtime distinguished professor of the humanities at CUNY's College of Staten Island, Schulman is now the Ralla Klepak Professor of English at Northwestern University, where she teaches creative writing. The interviews collected here make it clear that Schulman relishes dialogue in any setting—with students, professional journalists, fellow writers, and even with adversaries. Conversation is a key component of Schulman's life. It is one of her gifts.

It has been a pleasure to work once again with the University Press of Mississippi. I wish to thank my editor, Mary Heath, and the many friends who either read parts of the manuscript or talked with me about the project as it took shape—Franklin Cham, Laura Dubek, Sara Dunne, Graham Grubb, Jill Hague, Marion Hollings, Mark Islam, Angelo Pitillo, and Jon Witherspoon. And I am grateful to Middle Tennessee State University's College of Graduate Studies and its Department of English for generously underwriting the final costs of permissions to reprint.

WB

Notes

1. J. P. Der Boghossian, host, "Facing the Homophobia in Our Families with Barrak Alzaid and Sarah Schulman," *This Queer Book Saved My Life!*, February 7, 2023, season 2, episode 19, https://thisqueerbook.com/podcast/ties-that-bind/.

2. Ezra Klein, host, "Sarah Schulman's Radical Approach to Conflict, Communication and Change," *The Ezra Klein Show*, audio podcast, *New York Times*, June 22, 2021, https://www.nytimes.com/2021/06/22/opinion/ezra-klein-podcast-sarah-schulman.html. In addition to the printed interviews provided in this collection, readers should seek out the podcasts on which Schulman has frequently appeared. See https://www.owltail.com/people/LVhyS-sarah-schulman/appearances.

Chronology

1958–1979　Born in New York City; sees plays at the Yiddish theater on Second Avenue with her grandmother, an Eastern European immigrant (Austro-Hungarian Empire). Attends Hunter College High School and enters the University of Chicago but drops out after an arrest for protesting the university's decision to honor Robert S. McNamara with an international relations award.

1979–1982　Participates in an abortion underground railroad between Spain and France and becomes active in the Committee for Abortion Rights and Against Sterilization Abuse (CARASA); takes part in a "zap" action that disrupts a congressional anti-abortion hearing and is convicted of disruption of Congress. Receives a bachelor of arts in cultural studies from SUNY, Empire State College, which includes study with Audre Lorde at Hunter College. Works as a waitress at Leroy's, a Tribeca coffee shop. Enrolls in a master's program at CUNY, City College of New York, but is advised by Grace Paley to pursue her own writing rather than an advanced degree. Begins career as a journalist at the newly founded *Womanews*, a New York City feminist newspaper.

1983　Writes for *Gay Community News*, the *New York Native*, and, later, the *Village Voice*.

1984　Publishes first novel, *The Sophie Horowitz Story* (Naiad Press), and becomes a notable voice in the then-budding genre of lesbian crime fiction. Awarded Fulbright Fellowship in Judaic Studies.

1986　Publishes *Girls, Visions and Everything: A Novel* (Seal Press), focusing on lesbian friendships in New York's Lower East Side in the 1980s. Awarded the first of twelve MacDowell residencies.

1987　Joins the AIDS Coalition to Unleash Power (ACT UP) and establishes, with filmmaker Jim Hubbard, the New York Lesbian and Gay Experimental Film Festival (MIX NYC), which

	continues for thirty-three years. Receives the first of three fellowships from the New York Foundation for the Arts (Fiction, 1987 and 1991; Playwriting/Screenwriting, 2006).
1988	Publishes *After Delores* (Dutton; 25th anniversary edition by Arsenal Pulp Press, 2013). A noir-inspired treatment of lesbian subculture, Schulman's entry into mainstream publishing is compared favorably with Jay McInerney's *Bright Lights, Big City* (1984) and Bret Easton Ellis's *Less than Zero* (1985). Receives the American Library Association's Stonewall Book Award for Fiction (1989).
1990	Publishes *People in Trouble* (Dutton; Vintage edition, 2019), which makes AIDS and people affected by the disease a major focus of its narrative, and which depicts, indirectly, the ACT UP activism that would become a lynchpin in Schulman's subsequent career.
1992	Publishes *Empathy* (Dutton; Arsenal Pulp Press, 2006), a fictional challenge to Freud's theory of the Elektra complex. Arsenal's "Little Sister's Classics" reprint contains Schulman's self-reflective essay "What I've Learned about *Empathy*." Cofounds the Lesbian Avengers, a direct-action group that used creative tactics to combat legalized discrimination and advance lesbian interests.
1994	Publishes *My American History: Lesbian and Gay Life during the Reagan/Bush Years* (Routledge; 2nd edition 2019), an expansive collection of early journalism from *Off Our Backs*, *Out Week*, *Womanews*, and other periodicals. Includes "When We Were Very Young: A Walking Tour through Radical Jewish Women's History on the Lower East Side, 1879–1919" and excerpts from *The Lesbian Avenger Handbook*.
1995	Publishes *Rat Bohemia* (Dutton; Arsenal Pulp Press edition, 2008). Often cited as Schulman's signature novel, *Rat Bohemia* is praised in the *New York Times Book Review* by Edmund White: "The force of her indignation is savage and has blown the traditional novel off its hinges. If she were contributing to the [AIDS Memorial] quilt, her quilt would be on fire." Named a top 100 gay novel by both the Publishing Triangle and the *New York Times*.
1996	Appears in Cheryl Dunne's *The Watermelon Woman*, a fictional film about a Black actress who plays Mammy figures in

	American films of the 1930s. Awarded the first of four residencies at Yaddo.
1997	Publishes *Collected Early Novels of Sarah Schulman: The Sophie Horowitz Story*; *Girls, Visions and Everything*; *After Delores* (Quality Paperback Book Club); and *Promenade*, a play, in *Intimate Acts: 8 Contemporary Lesbian Plays* (Brito and Lair). Appears as a commentator in Paris Poirier's documentary *Pride Divide*, the first of several appearances in documentaries on gay and lesbian culture, including *Little Sister's vs. Big Brother* (2002), *Video Remains* (2005), *Queer Realities and Cultural Amnesia* (2005), *Hooters!* (2010), and *Dykes, Camera, Action!* (2018).
1998	Publishes *Shimmer* (Perennial), a novel with three interlocking narrators whose lives are marked by the rise of McCarthyism, and *Stagestruck: Theater, AIDS, and the Marketing of Gay America* (Duke University Press), detailing the ways in which her 1990 novel *People in Trouble* served as an uncredited but major source for *Rent*, the hit Broadway play by Jonathan Larson. Highlighting the commodification of gay and lesbian culture by mainstream artists, producers, and publishers, *Stagestruck* receives the American Library Association's Stonewall Book Award for Nonfiction (1999).
1999	Begins teaching at CUNY, College of Staten Island, where she becomes distinguished professor in 2010.
2001	Initiates, with Jim Hubbard, the ACT UP Oral History Project, which ultimately provides 187 interviews with original ACT UP activists, including—to name just five—Mark Harrington, Larry Kramer, Ann Northrop, Peter Staley, and Maxine Wolfe. The interviews are made available to the public for free through transcripts and video clips at actuporalhistory.org. Receives a Guggenheim Fellowship in Playwrighting.
2002	Contributes to *Heaven and Hell (On Earth): A Divine Comedy*, a collection of scenes and monologues staged at the Actors Theatre of Louisville, Humana Festival. *Carson McCullers (Historically Inaccurate)*, developed at the Sundance Theatre Lab, is performed at Playwrights Horizons, New York (published by Playscripts, Inc., 2006). Directed by Marion McClinton, the play depicts pivotal moments in the life of Schulman's favorite fiction writer.

2003   *The Burning Deck*, starring Diane Venora, is performed in the Page to Stage program at the La Jolla Playhouse, California.
2005   *Manic Flight Reaction*, staring Deirdre O'Connell, is performed at Playwrights Horizons, New York.
2007   *Enemies, A Love Story*, adapted from the 1966 novel of the same name by Isaac Bashevis Singer, and staring Morgan Spector, is performed at the Wilma Theater as part of the Philadelphia New Play Festival: Where Theatre Begins. Publishes *The Child* (Carroll & Graf; Arsenal Pulp Press edition, 2008). Schulman attempts for years, without success, to publish this novel about an intergenerational relationship that ends tragically. She cites it as a personal favorite of her books.
2008   Awarded New York Institute of the Humanities Fellowship.
2009   Publishes *The Mere Future* (Arsenal Pulp Press), a dystopian and experimental novel that blends political commentary with satire, and *Ties That Bind: Familial Homophobia and Its Consequences* (New Press; reprint edition 2012), which argues that family structures themselves sustain homophobia. Publishes *Mercy*, a play (Belladonna Books). Named by *Utne Reader* as one of "50 Visionaries Who Will Change Your World" and by *Out* magazine as one of the one hundred most significant contributors to the LGBT community. Receives the Modern Language Association's LGBT/Michael Lynch Service Award and the Center for LGBTQ Kessler Award for a body of work that has influenced the field of gay and lesbian studies. Declines an invitation to speak at Tel Aviv University, in order to show solidarity with the Boycott, Divestment, and Sanctions movement in support of Palestine.
2010   Cowrites screenplay for Cheryl Dunne's film *The Owls*, a Berlin Film Festival selection. Organizes a US tour of Queer Palestinian Leaders.
2011   Receives a Brown Foundation Fellowship from the Museum of Fine Arts, Houston, Texas.
2012   Publishes *The Gentrification of the Mind: Witness to a Lost Imagination* (University of California Press). Part memoir and part cultural critique, the book links gentrification with the AIDS crisis and cements Shulman's reputation as a cultural provocateur. Cowrites the screenplay for a second feature film by Cheryl Dunne, *Mommy Is Coming*, another Berlin Film

Festival selection. Coproduces *United in Anger: A History of ACT UP*, a documentary film directed by Jim Hubbard, featuring archival footage and interviews with multiple participants in ACT UP. Publishes *Israel/Palestine and the Queer International* (Duke University Press). Following a controversial op-ed in the *New York Times*, Schulman argues that the state of Israel's support of gays and lesbians "pinkwashes" its oppression of Palestinians and is barred temporarily from promoting the book at New York's LGBT Community Center. Named to Advisory Board of Jewish Voice for Peace; coordinates the first US LGBT Delegation to Palestine.

2013 Organizes the conference "Homonationalsm and Pinkwashing," Center for LGBTQ Studies, CUNY Graduate Center.

2015 Cowrites and performs in *Jason and Shirley*, a feature film inspired by Shirley Clarke's 1967 documentary *Portrait of Jason*, about a Black gay male prostitute. Premieres at the Brooklyn Academy of Music and plays at the Museum of Modern Art.

2016 Faces allegations of anti-Semitism from the Zionist Organization of America; testifies and rebuts charges before a CUNY task force. Publishes *The Cosmopolitans* (Feminist Press at CUNY), which depicts the rift in a friendship between a Black closeted gay man and a white spinster who are Greenwich Village neighbors in 1958. First conceived as a play, the book was inspired by Honoré de Balzac's *Cousin Bette* (1846) and James Baldwin's *Another Country* (1962). Selected by *Publishers Weekly* as one of the best novels of 2016. Publishes *Conflict Is Not Abuse: Overstating Harm, Community Responsibility, and the Duty of Repair* (Arsenal Pulp Press), which presents Schulman's distinctions between abuse as an exercise of power over others and conflict as a potentially creative power struggle between people. The book sells over forty thousand copies and prompts many requests for interviews.

2018 Publishes *Maggie Terry* (Feminist Press at CUNY). Schulman's eleventh novel brings together social realism and lesbian crime fiction, a genre that she pioneered. Presented with the Publishing Triangle's Bill Whitehead Award for lifetime achievement

2021 Publishes *Let the Record Show: A Political History of ACT UP, New York, 1987–1993* (Farrar, Straus and Giroux), recipient of the Lambda Book Award in Nonfiction, and finalist for the PEN/John Kenneth Galbraith Award for Nonfiction and the Gotham Book Prize for Best New York City–based book, among other honors. Drawing from her interviews with ACT UP activists conducted over eighteen years, Schulman provides an encompassing history of the twentieth century's last great social movement while demonstrating the map it provides for continued social change. Awarded the Ann Snitow Prize for a visionary feminist thinker who enhances the intellectual life of her time.

2022   *The Lady Hamlet* is performed at the Provincetown Theater, Massachusetts, and receives the BroadwayWorld Boston Prize for Best New Play. Awarded the Ralla Klepak Professorship in English at Northwestern University, Evanston, Illinois.

Conversations with
Sarah Schulman

New Faces

Karla Jay / 1988

From *Village Voice*, June 28, 1988, 24–26. Reprinted with permission.

Though the nameless narrator of Sarah Schulman's *After Delores* is supposedly on the trail of whoever murdered go-go dancer Punkette, the novel really delineates a lesbian's obsession with Delores, the woman who abandoned her for someone newer and richer. Although Delores remains primarily offstage, she is the object of the narrator's fantasies of violence and revenge. As Schulman puts it, "I think that when you are very angry and you've experienced loss, or a sense of betrayal, your view of the world becomes very skewed. Anger is hallucinatory...."

After Delores explores the dark sides of passion, sleazy and negative emotions some of us hope to leave safely in the closet. Schulman may be the first to sound the death knell for the "good girl" lesbian novel and foreshadow a new permission to explore steaminess as well as glory. Is this the new lesbian aesthetic? How will we appear to the world when this is how we appear in our books?

Karla Jay: Is there a problem with presenting violence by lesbians in a book that's going to be read by heterosexuals?

Sarah Schulman: I don't have a problem with it. I know that other people have a problem because they're afraid that heterosexuals will use this information against us. It's a very defensive position, and I don't want to behave defensively in my writing. I'm interested in presenting lesbians in their total humanity, which includes everything that every other person is allowed. I just absolutely refuse to be controlled in that way. I mean the angry young man is a total classic in literature. How come we're not allowed to do that?

You know, bigots are bigots. So for me to talk about real people and real feelings, if that makes some homophobes feel they're justified, well, that's their problem. We can't distort and corrupt gay culture to adapt to bigotry. That's totally the wrong thing to do. You know, that's like saying Alice Walker shouldn't have written *The Color Purple* because she says such bad things about Black men. I am a writer and I have the right to write my worldview.

Jay: Is what you're doing part of a trend or do you see yourself working in isolation?

Schulman: I'm twenty-nine years old. When I came into puberty, there was already a gay movement. I'm part of the first generation that had that. And I think a lot of people my age, in many other fields—if you look at popular music, whatever—have never been in the closet their entire lives, and also have not had to put up with the stigmatization that the generation before us had to. So we have one foot firmly planted in gay culture, which has always been there for us, and one foot in popular culture, which makes for a very different blend, and a very different perspective. And so you're seeing young lesbians presenting their work in the mainstream, who don't hide their sexuality. In that sense, the lesbian aesthetic is changing.

Jay: When we talk about lesbian aesthetics, is there a uniform sensibility or are there, for example, regional gaps?

Schulman: Well, there are great gaps aesthetically. That's the problem, because lesbian work has been so repressed for so long the quality of the work and the level of discourse are not very high. I know that when I first started, I wanted to write books that assumed the lesbian perspective, that assumed lesbianism was normal and used that as the starting point for a worldview: books that were not about coming out. But as I've been writing, I've gotten more and more interested in putting words together, structuring a novel, and I find that the kind of discussion I need is very hard to find in the lesbian community. It's not impossible to find in San Francisco or New York, but once you get off the coasts, you cannot get anything—comments, discussion, questions—that are helpful to me.

Jay: It seems that more and more lesbian novels are put out by alternative presses, like Naiad, Firebrand, and Seal Press, but there are fewer and fewer books by major publishers.

Schulman: Actually, I think it's opening up a lot. My book is doing really well, and that's going to help other lesbian novels. The small presses and gay bookstores have created a market, and publishers, all they really care about is money. They're not publishing me because they love homosexuals, or anything like that. So here's this lesbian market with extremely loyal readers, who really care about the writers and who are willing to buy these books. Plus there are more visible gay people in publishing.

Jay: Where do you go from here?

Schulman: I have a new novel called *People in Trouble*. It's about AIDS activism. None of the protagonists has AIDS. It's about living in a city where you're carrying on the little melodramas of your personal life, and as you're walking down the street, every five minutes someone is asking you for money, and someone you know is in the hospital, and you're always going to a funeral, and someone is always homeless in front of your apartment. But still your life goes on.

A Conversation with Sarah Schulman

Christi Cassidy / 1989

From *Visibilities: The Lesbian Magazine*, January/February 1989, 8–11.
Used by permission of the author.

Wearing a gray Amelia Earhart–style jumpsuit over a black T-shirt, Sarah Schulman slouches in an overstuffed easy chair, grimacing over each question posed to her. There are long silences between the questions and her answers, as if through pondering she is in fact unraveling the world's great mysteries. An infectious laugh—nearly two octaves higher than her speaking voice—punctuates her comments, making her seem less the brooding social critic.

While contemporary social issues permeate the conversation, Schulman begins with, and focuses on, the process of writing, literature, and *After Delores*. "Delores is the narrator's no-good girlfriend who walked out on her for a yuppie. Delores isn't that present in the book, but she's the motivating force for the action and feeling that take place."

The narrator is unnamed because, Schulman says, "Taking away her name took away her ethnicity." For a writer who's admired for her sassy, Jewish protagonists, this choice served to obliterate the Jewish lesbian voice. "I couldn't write the Jewish character without being really funny. I didn't want to be that funny this time. . . . Later, people told me it was funny anyway. It's deadpan humor."

Sarah Schulman is perhaps best known for her first novel, *The Sophie Horowitz Story*, published in 1984 by Naiad Press. Since then, she's penned two novels, with a third on the way, and numerous play adaptations, performance pieces, and nonfiction newspaper articles.

Already into its second printing, *After Delores*, published in 1988 by E. P. Dutton, marks her first venture into commercial publishing. Rave reviews from the *New York Times*, *Publishers Weekly*, *Gay Community News* in Boston, *Kirkus Reviews*, and *The News* from Southern California, testify to her wide audience appeal. New American Library has purchased the paperback rights and there's talk of film adaptation.

Schulman claims her past books—*The Sophie Horowitz Story* and *Girls, Visions and Everything*—were "easily dismissed" because they were not only funny but characterized as "genre novels." Stripping away the ethnicity freed her "to talk about *lesbian* experience, which is not discussed ever except by a handful of people, then talk about gentrification, and then talk about, on the human level, how horrible it is when you love someone so much and then you hate them . . . I was frustrated and I wanted people to see that my work, was really serious. So I took away the clown."

After Delores is essentially a mystery, with the slow degeneration of the main character at its heart. Alcoholism, lost love, anger, murderous urges, violence between women, and intergenerational lesbian love are all issues touched upon with compassion and even humor. Schulman makes writing look simple: moments of tenderness and poignancy indent her fast-paced dialogue and action. "Any person can read my books," she asserts. "You don't have to have gone to college. You don't have to know poetry or art." Her characters are recognizable, with ambitions of their own and a certain familiarity that puts the reader right at home.

Home for Schulman is New York City's Lower East Side—a melting pot of street people, yuppies, drug dealers, theatre types, and young innocents. Schulman excels at bringing out her colorful street language and life that surround her. "These characters are archetypes but no one knows it but us because they're not archetypes in literature. . . . In life we know these types of women. When people respond to my books, they always say, 'Oh, I know that type—it's the falling-in-love-with-a-straight-woman thing.'"

Schulman does not, however, view herself as a scribe for the lesbian community. "I see myself primarily as a social critic," she says quietly. "I don't think any of this will survive time. In fact, the first book is already outdated and it's only been four years."

As a social critic, she sees herself in a long tradition of New York intellectuals, beginning with Delmore Schwartz and running through Philip Roth and Woody Allen. "I'm a woman and a lesbian and a leftist and I'm doing exactly what they do. . . . Of course, none of them has ever heard of me!" She laughs, then continues, "I hope that someday if this discrimination against lesbians goes away that, later, people will be able to see that."

All her characters reveal aspects of herself and, Schulman swears, all the events in her novels are true. Regarding *After Delores*, though, she admits there was no murder per se, nor is she an alcoholic. In all her writing, she tries to "get away from the generalizations." Specificity extends to the subject of violence against women as well. The main character carries a gun given to her and struggles with the temptations its presence offers. "When I was having the experiences upon which this book is based," Schulman says, "I realized that if I had a weapon in my house, somebody would now be dead."

The "old gay" code of honor compels Schulman. "I would say the narrator's basic moral argument is that, if you take something away from somebody you have to give them something back. . . . If you're going to dump somebody, you have to let them be angry. If you're going to walk out on somebody, you have to give them the apartment.'"

As she talks about anger, moving from the specifics of her book into theory, Schulman tenses; her face becomes a mask of seriousness. "The early lesbian community was much more aggressive, brave, critical, individual, and creative than it is now. I don't think it was rigid or closed at all. . . . The *theory* was angry! . . . Adrienne Rich's 'Compulsory Homosexuality' is an article that totally transformed my life. . . . It is fantastic! Nothing like that could be written today because there is a degree of anger that is used in such a creative manner, and that anger has become forbidden. When you read lesbian writing today, it's just not there."

She concedes that "we have the Reagan era and a lot of lesbian stuff has become depoliticized." Modes of oppression and ostracism have changed. "The way of being diminished has changed so that women and lesbians are still diminished, socially, but in a much more insidious manner. Before, lesbian identity was completely defined by the underground. Now, it's in *People Magazine*. That's not positive. It's good to be out there but the image is not a good one. . . . So there seems to be more acceptance, but when it's done in mass media, the radical critique is absent." Without the political and socioeconomic analysis, Schulman feels the image of women, specifically lesbians, is distorted.

Since lesbians are only beginning to address social issues in their novels, the second step is to explore the texture of their inner lives. Schulman compares lesbian literary evolution to that of Black novelists. "Books like Claude Brown's *Manchild in the Promised Land* and other Black, socially active classics of that period are about the economic conflict of Black people in a white world. Books that were written more recently, like *The Color Purple* or *The Women of Brewster Place*, are about the richness of the interior life. I'm trying to do both at the same time. When you're discussing the interior life, you have all the dimensions of human experience, including betrayal and loss of faith.

"The best books being written now by lesbians are not overtly lesbian," she continues. "For example, *Ghost Dance* by Carole Maso and *Water Dancer* by Jenifer Levin are wonderfully written. The lesbian issues are secondary."

At age thirty, Schulman already has the writing and publishing experience to give her unique insight into the progress of lesbian writing. "I grew up with the gay movement. It's marked me forever." She adds, "An advantage to lesbian writers a little bit younger than me is that they have an integrated sense of themselves in the world. It used to be that you never discussed your gay life, your lover, with even your best friend. Now, you can write a book about lesbians that takes place in popular culture because you *live* in popular culture."

Schulman relates a wry story that led her to an important career decision. "When I was at the MacDowell Artists Colony two years ago, three gay writers sat me down at a table and said, 'Sarah, you will never get a commercial publisher if you continue to have only gay primary characters.' One said, 'You can have your fabulous fags and your fabulous dykes, but you have to have a few blahs.'" She doubles over, laughing. "But they've been wrong. Totally wrong. I knew I was not going to do anything they suggested.

"At some point I made a decision to reveal everything about myself and I learned that you can do that and people still don't know you. It's not as frightening as people think because all you're really revealing is your commonality with other people.

"That is what I think good fiction is," she says. "I believe that plot is basically a device—and my books are very plot-heavy. I don't believe in plot. If you're a great writer—like Proust, Kerouac, or Jane Bowles—you don't need plot because the emotions, the honesty, the integrity overcome that need."

She frequently interrupts the conversation to assert that she is "not a very skilled writer," and in fact, she had never met a writer until after her second book was published. "I had never written a short story, never taken a creative writing class. I was a waitress!"

In 1980, after having been away from the city, she returned to New York and called up a friend, who invited her to "come start a newspaper." At *Womanews*—the end result of that meeting—she discovered a penchant for journalism. After the Brinks trial, she realized that there was a story that couldn't be captured in a newspaper piece and "sat down and wrote a novel."

Currently laboring over a novel about AIDS, Schulman insists that "AIDS is a subject that fiction won't encompass. My skill is not such that fiction can encompass the enormity of that experience." She takes a sip of her beer; a pained look crosses her face. "But I never read a book about the Holocaust that portrayed what it really was. Talk about rape can never convey the horror of it. I'm avoiding trying to sum up the enormity of it."

Through the AIDS Coalition to Unleash Power (ACT UP) in New York, Schulman fulfills her need "to work for freedom." She says, "I used to be much more politically active before I started writing and now that I've gotten involved in the AIDS movement, I want to get back to that. It's more important."

Will she continue writing? "No," she states, looking out the window and lighting a cigarette. "Writing novels is too lonely. It takes a year or two years . . . it's very solitary. No one knows what I'm doing. I'd like to work on things that involve collaboration because I've been very frustrated by how politically ineffective writing is.

"When artists say to me, 'My artwork is political work,' I want to vomit. Because artists can do their artwork and then they have to make a stand with everybody else—stuff envelopes and stand on picket lines and disrupt things. You have to do that. Sitting home and writing does not do that."

Fury flashes in her brown eyes. "AIDS can't be understood. That all your friends are dying at the age of thirty? And the government is letting them? It's unbelievable! There's so much disgrace involved in this issue that it can't be conveyed."

The irony, she concedes, is that the gay community is perhaps the most well equipped to deal with an epidemic like AIDS because gay people are used to taking care of themselves, not expecting anyone else to care for them.

"The tricky dichotomy for the gay writer," Shulman points out, "is presenting a person who, on the one hand, is human and flawed, and on the other hand has found a degree of individual strength that many other people in the world lack. That's the challenge."

She writes out of the conflicts in her life and hopes in five years "to be a little happier. When I'm happy I can't write. I'd like to be so happy I don't want to write. When I'm old I'd like to write my memoirs and have them be called *Paradise Now*." Her staccato laugh fills the room.

"I should be writing because that's what I *want* to do, not because I have to. I don't want to be a hack."

Sarah Schulman

Milyoung Cho / 1993

This interview, *Sarah Schuman by Milyoung Cho*, was commissioned by and first published in *BOMB* no. 42, Winter 1993. © *BOMB Magazine*, New Art Publications, and its Contributors. All rights reserved. The *BOMB* Digital Archive can be viewed at www.bombmagazine.org.

Sarah Schulman does not hesitate to commit a "cultural violation." She constantly transgresses the boundaries of what is expected of her: as a writer, as an activist, as a white lesbian living in America. Her fifth and latest novel, *Empathy* (Dutton), sputters social realist doses of a crisis-ridden, morally bankrupt New York. Stumbling over the gritty urban terrain, her sensitive but righteous characters search for their own place while struggling internally around gender and sexuality. As an activist with ACT UP and the emerging Lesbian Avengers, Schulman boldly embraces in-your-face direct-action tactics. For their first action, the new group responded to a Queens school board ban on mentioning homosexuality until the eighth grade by handing out balloons to elementary school students emblazoned with the suggestion: "Ask About Lesbians."

Milyoung Cho: Do your writing and your political work have anything to do with each other, or are they two separate parts of your life?

Sarah Schulman: The fiction is about politics, but not because I decided it would be but because that's my worldview. I don't have any illusions that my fiction writing is making any social changes. There's a lot of rhetoric going around about telling your story as "an act of resistance." I really don't think that that's true. Writing is what I love to do the most. It's an extremely pleasurable experience, plus I get a lot of approval for it. It's hardly an act of resistance; it's become a completely contained action. I write a book and a corporate publisher publishes it and the media reviews it. It's been commodified and contained. I enjoy it, and if people reading it enjoy it, that's good. But I have no illusion that that's a substitute for organizing. If you use personal success as a substitute for political achievement, you're not moving forward as a community and you're not building political power, which is what our community needs.

MC: In the sixties and seventies, communities of antiestablishment people were called the counterculture as if they were perpetually reacting. We always have to react to dominant, oppressive forces and systems. Do you feel that this sets up your writing?

SS: In the eighties there was an experiment in lesbian fiction about trying to create a world in which the objective, neutral, and authoritative voice was a lesbian voice. That was about trying to see the world from our points of view. In each person's point of view, they are central. How do we articulate that in a context in which we are invisible and meaningless? People did try and I tried too. But after all these years of being punished, watching our friends drop dead and seeing what's happened in our country . . . it's been so dramatic and so dehumanizing that a lot of lesbian work has become about being marginal. I have a review that came out in *Publishers Weekly*, and the first words are "Lesbian writer." I don't have a problem with that, but they could say Jewish writer, or comic writer, or political writer, or whatever. Your marginality becomes your primary identity. I'm really trapped in this struggle with marginality and my resentments about it. It's the thing that I look at the most, and many of my insights are about that state. If you are a really enlightened person, sometimes you can get through that. But right now, my subject matter is the separation, and the exclusion, even though I try to be funny about it.

MC: I was thinking about the character Anna and how her homophobic ex-lover describes her as narrow because she is gay . . .

SS: I talk about this all of the time with gay writers, lesbian writers: we are not invited into the intellectual discourse of this nation. We are never asked about anything unless it's a gay topic. But I have a very wide range of things to say from my lesbian perspective, about what's going on in America's culture. We have been incredibly abused by the television—with the Republican convention and all that crap. One reason being that the vast majority of gay people who are in the media are invisible and closeted. And once you are not closeted you become dehumanized and devalued. Your word becomes "special interest" and "extremist." You can no longer be of interest to the dominant culture. The most powerful and gifted people in our community are closeted. We have a brain drain of credibility. The most famous woman intellectual in the world, the most prominent Black woman political leader in this country, the greatest Latina playwright in America, a prominent choreographer . . . all of these people are recognized as smart and brilliant women and yet are complicit with the lie that to be a brilliant and creative woman you must give up sex and love. There's a glass wall between "us" and "them." They fear that if they come out they will lose their credibility, no matter how much they have achieved.

MC: Does this lay an extra burden on the creative people who are out to explore those things that people in the closet wouldn't even touch?

SS: Yes, but it doesn't matter how much we achieve because legitimacy isn't there for us. Look at Alice Walker's *The Color Purple*. You could say that is a piece of lesbian literature because the character is transformed through a sexual relationship with another woman, but the popular discourse couldn't contain that. So, even when the quality of a piece is broadly recognized, the lesbianism often conveniently disappears from the discourse.

MC: Do you identify as a lesbian writer?

SS: Yes.

MC: I was looking at the word "empathy" in the dictionary and they had a psychological definition, "It is the power to enter into the spirit of others." What does empathy mean for you?

SS: The original title was *Empathy, The Cheapest of Emotions*. It was about being liberal. But so much has happened in this country in the past three years that even asking for empathy is asking for more than what is possible. [*Laughter*] So I changed the title. Mostly I was thinking about AIDS and the lack of respect and compassion, and the neglect that America has exhibited. Even something as banal as empathy doesn't exist in the way America views gay people.

MC: The situation is so bad now that we don't have the luxury to deride liberalism.

SS: I have been really active on the Oregon antigay initiative this past week. Do you know about that Black lesbian and gay white male who were burned to death in their home by skinheads? Their names are Hattie Mae Cohens and Brian Mock. There is not one word about these killings in the national media. This should be like the Bumpers case or the Emmett Till case. But the message is gay people's lives mean nothing. I keep wondering who is gonna do something about this, and then you start calling around and finding that no one is really in charge. The previous model for social change has been revolution, everyone has sat around for a really long time and said, "When the revolution comes dadadadada. . . ." It ends up being a very disempowering model because revolution isn't coming. The message that it really sends is that unless total social transformation comes, you can't act. But you can do one act of resistance every day. Every day step out of your role, do something you wouldn't normally do to try and have an effect.

MC: What do you mean, step out of your role?

SS: You have to commit a cultural violation. In our community, cultural production has become a substitute for political work. People can go to a reading and see this multicultural production, but when they leave that room, nothing has happened. They've had a "feel good" experience but it stopped there. Obviously, the status quo is killing us. So obviously, we aren't doing the right thing. We come away feeling good and two people still get killed in Oregon. And we're still not doing anything about it.

MC: In *Empathy*, Anna goes to Indonesia as a tourist. How does that relate to who she is socially?

SS: There has been a canonization of victimization in some corners, where a person has legitimacy if they are a victim, and that kind of role is very denying of what it is to be an American. I learned something about this in ACT UP. A lot of the men there are very clear on how they are being fucked over by the government, by the heterosexual establishment, by the pharmaceutical corporations, but they have no consciousness about other people who have AIDS and who don't have what they have, and their responsibility to them. My characters, Anna and Doc, in the framework of New York City, are not very powerful, but they can still be international tourists in a Third World country. They can come with a "noble savage" metaphor and have it broken and be shocked that it's broken, and then see it as a metaphor for themselves as broken. The way white people in our community have traditionally glorified and then canonized the culture they are entering—"those people are so spiritual; their country is so beautiful."

MC: I've been in that situation myself. Even though I am Asian, I could very well be someone like Anna. When I was in Thailand, I was always very self-conscious about my presence. At the same time, I also felt a lot of outrage about what other tourists were doing. There were all these white American and European men hounding these Thai boys all around the country. Seeing these levels of tourist exploitation, I always had to question how I fit into the whole scene.

SS: Imperialism cannot be avoided, and it's very shocking to discover that, because a lot of people are under the illusion that it can.

MC: It seems that we are so caught up in the crisis at hand that there is no room for us to talk about vision and where we see ourselves heading. Is this how you see it?

SS: Yes. And we haven't created our own space, we have no lesbian media. I've been interviewed hundreds of times; every person who has interviewed me, before you, has been white. The gay media is so insanely segregated that it is useless. You have these magazines with all-white editorial staff who are content having a circulation of five to eight thousand white males and don't care about serving the rest of the community or raising their circulation. We have cultural events and readings but no place to really talk about anything. A sort of rejection of dissent gets put into play passively, because of the lack of public debate. We don't have access to mainstream media either. But I don't think creating more underground press is the issue here. For some reason the community has not been able to confront the white press and force change.

MC: Do you feel we would be better off struggling from the margins in a predominantly white straight media, rather than creating our own?

SS: We are having this conversation because of *BOMB Magazine*, not because of *Out* or *QW* or *The Advocate*. I think groups like the Gay and Lesbian Alliance Against Defamation should be going after the gay media and saying to them that an all-white editorial staff is not acceptable. They give a distorted view of gay life.

MC: It's about holding our own community accountable. What do you do about it?

SS: One simple thing that white people can do in this community is, if you're an artist, refuse to be in a program that's racially segregated. Just say you won't. Those programs will not continue if enough people say that. It's a little thing that can actually have a huge impact. If I'm going to have work in an anthology, I try to find out if it's going to have a really diverse group of writers contributing and whether people are being tokenized. I can't have an illusion that my white editor, who is my age and is a lesbian, just happens to think that I'm the best writer. When actually there's a whole issue of sociological identification and familiarity going on. There is no out Asian lesbian editor who is bringing in writers in the same way. Look at Audre Lorde. Here's this person that a lot of people will tell you is the most important writer in their life. A book like *Zami* changed people's lives. She was never published by a mainstream press; she was never reviewed in the *New York Times* for fiction writing. What's the reason? Why do I have a corporate publisher and she didn't? It's not like I'm a better writer than Audre Lorde. That's obviously not the issue.

MC: What are you saying about your own writing when you're saying this?

SS: I'm trying to keep aware of what it really means and doesn't mean. And in what context and compared to whom. When I'm in a room of all men, it has a different meaning, and when I'm in the lesbian community, who I am is different again. What do you think about not having a static identity?

MC: That's just a part of my life. People will perceive me based on all kinds of cultural information in one world, but when I'm at home with my family . . . well, not my family, that's a whole other issue. [*Laughter*] But within the Asian community, it's something very different. It's not something I even think about too much.

SS: There's probably no one on this earth whose parent, you know, when they were born, thought, "Oh, I hope she'll grow up and become a lesbian writer." [*Laughter*] The profound rejection that gay people have had from their families is often the most important event in our lives—not just individually but as a community. Who's fighting for civil rights of gay people? Only gay people. Who's fighting for our cultural production? Only we are. We've had to step into the role of family and the role of mutual aid society and the role of everything. We provide counseling services; we provide street patrols. We've had to provide everything because the America that is our families has abandoned us. It's a very profound rejection and it forms us as a community.

MC: Your character Anna is definitely in that situation. She doesn't have a sense of who she is—being told she wants to be a man but that she hates them at the same time. She does come to some wholeness at the end. Do you feel like there is some possibility for us? [*Laughter*]

SS: We are each other's knights in shining armor. Let's face it, nobody else is going to come along and rescue us.

Sarah Schulman: "I'm There Because I Have Certain Beliefs"

Kate Brandt / 1993

From *Happy Endings: Lesbian Writers Talk about Their Lives and Work*, Naiad Press, 1993. Reprinted with the permission of Donna J. McBride for Naiad Press.

"When I meet people—for example, to do an interview—they usually will comment on how they are surprised that I'm so serious and intellectual," Sarah Schulman offers. "Because from reading the books, they expect a raucous alcoholic or something."

"The books" are Schulman's five novels to date, thought-provoking stories "about being marginal, about being invisible, about getting lost," as she describes them. While her central characters are lesbians, her books "are not about coming out. There are a lot of issues that are connected to the characters' lesbianism. But the books are not about transforming into the lesbian identity."

Schulman began her writing career as a journalist, working for the New York City–based feminist newspaper *Womanews*. "I wrote for every issue of *Womanews* for five years," she recalls. "That's where I learned how to write about a community for that same community, which is really challenging. The very people you're writing about are the people reading it, and if they detect some kind of voyeurism or lack of sincerity, they let you know right away.

"Writing for the movement press was all about learning description, listening carefully to what people were saying, trying to detect trends. Also, you have the advantage of seeing your work published right away. It's a really good place to learn how to write."

Schulman's first attempt at fiction became her first published novel, *The Sophie Horowitz Story* (1984), which recounts the adventures of a lesbian journalist who is fascinated with a radical fugitive. "I had interviewed these women who were involved with the infamous Weather Underground

Brink's robbery in the early 1980s," Schulman explains about *Sophie*'s origins. "And their stories were so incredible to me that I just started having fantasies about them and writing stories about them."

Schulman's second book, *Girls, Visions and Everything* (1986), follows "dyke about town" Lila Futuransky through a summer on New York's Lower East Side. Of *Girls*, Schulman says, "I was interested in the 'lesbian boyhood,' where a girl places herself in the kind of imaginative adventure fiction that's traditionally reserved for boys. I had identified with these writers like Jack Kerouac, and the only way you could enjoy his books was if you were Jack. If you identified with the women in the book, you couldn't enjoy it. 'Lesbian boyhood' was something that a lot of people have experienced, but it hadn't been articulated in fiction.

"When I toured with that book in 1988, I discovered that when I went to places where gay people felt safe, like San Francisco, they liked the book. When I went to places where gay people did not feel safe, they felt very threatened by the book, because they were still living with this fear that if you say that you do bad things and have bad feelings, straight people will use this against you. People will point to it and say, 'See, those people can't have healthy relationships.' It was like that fear of the dominant culture was keeping us from being complete people in our own fiction."

Schulman's most recent book, *Empathy* (1992), "a novel about how homophobia affects the female psychology," is "written in thought sentences," she explains. "So instead of being written in a conventional narrative style, it's written the way a person thinks. It's very loopy, and distracted, and fragmented; different ideas will set off other ideas.

"I allowed myself to work for two years without knowing what it was about," Schulman continues. "I just gave myself full permission to write. And when I finally realized what it was about, I was really glad I had given myself that permission, because what I found out was that I was writing totally from my unconscious. And therefore, it got much deeper, emotionally. So, I'm very, very happy with it."

It was [in] her fourth novel, *People in Trouble*, that Schulman confronted the subject that has cast the longest shadow on the contemporary gay movement: AIDS. At the time that the book was published in 1990, Schulman explained, "*People in Trouble* was [written] from an incredible need for this community to become activist again." She predicted that the book would be "outdated in three years. Because AIDS fiction is going to change and grow really fast. I think we're going to get to a place where we can write about AIDS in a more sophisticated manner. Because we're just beginning to start to write about AIDS, and we're going to be spending the rest of our lives trying to understand it."

Two years after making this statement, Schulman agrees with her own prediction, saying that "for the people who are having direct experience with AIDS and AIDS activism, *People in Trouble* may be outdated." But Schulman admits that her views on AIDS fiction have changed. "There was an expectation that AIDS would be a transformative experience, a moment of truth," she reflects. "And what I've found is that it's not true; people do *not* get transformed by having AIDS. They simply become themselves, just ever so much more so.

"And AIDS fiction—there was, I think, a burden placed on it where people expected the writers to have incredible insights into life and death, when actually the opposite has turned out to be true. AIDS fiction has become writing by people who don't feel well, who are depressed, who are writing against the clock and can't put as much time into it as they would like. And so a lot of the work has become rushed, incomplete, unsatisfying. What I'm realizing is that, instead of being revelatory, it's actually restricted. That's what AIDS fiction is, at this point: work in the face of enormous obstacles."

"Schulman sees her own writing of AIDS fiction as changed by factors that have evolved with the passage of time. "In *Empathy*, AIDS is treated very differently than it is in *People in Trouble*," Schulman points out, "because in my own life it's become normal. The experience of having someone talk to you about his impending death is now a normal experience that I have all the time. When I was writing *People in Trouble*, I was so shocked.

"I also did not anticipate how fully the government would try to obstruct every single action that people tried to initiate to impact on AIDS. It's been so demoralizing. So I think that demoralization and normalization are now what I'm writing about."

If gay men are not writing about AIDS as richly as was expected a few years ago, lesbian writers are not writing about the plague at all, according to Schulman. "I think lesbian writers are becoming more and more apolitical generally," she says. "I went to the Lambda Literary Awards last year [1991], and I was really shocked, because every other man who stood up talked about one who had died. And many women stood up and told really empty anecdotes about how they wrote their books.

"The larger world was not present. And I'm not just saying AIDS is the only thing; the collapse of the culture, the crisis of capitalism were not being directly addressed in many cases. Now, on the other hand, I think the quality of lesbian writing is improving," Schulman adds. "There have been some books published that are *excellent*, in terms of literary achievement. But they're not politicized. The lesbian writers are more politically conventional than they've ever been.

"When you take on the responsibility to be a writer, which is to be a public thinker, for a community that is dropping dead, basically, or is under siege—it shocks me that people take that position, to be a public thinker for a community in trouble, and then all they try to provide is entertainment. I don't understand how a person can do that.

"When you walk into a women's bookstore, and look at the lesbian section, most of the books are fairly pallid. They're not engaged with 'The World.' And that's very frustrating to me."

Schulman had her first lesbian relationship when she was sixteen years old, and she describes herself as a member of "the first generation that came out into an already existing gay movement [Schulman was born in 1958]. So when I was a teenager, there were already lesbian novels. *Rubyfruit Jungle* had already been published. This is the first time that we have a group of lesbians who are gay in popular culture, not separated from popular culture.

"Men and women living in both gay culture and popular culture are willingly participating in mixed communities. When I first came out, women's newspapers and organizations were very vibrant places, because there was a lot of discussion going on about how people were going to survive. That discussion is now taking place in a gay and lesbian context. We're seeing, more frequently, a switch to a co-ed community—a community of gay men and women together."

But in the past few years, many younger lesbian activists have become disillusioned working with gay men, and have become frustrated by the racism and sexism that they perceive within some cogender activist groups. Schulman, a self-described "rank-and-file member of ACT UP," acknowledges the existence of this conflict between lesbians and gay men. "The vast majority of gay men in ACT UP did not have reciprocal relationships with women, politically, socially, or personally," she points out. "And that is not because they're sick and dying, it's because they're men."

But although she admits that "[most gay men] really don't care about you, except in terms of what you mean to them," such sexism is not enough to discourage Schulman from remaining an activist. "That reality is not enough to determine my decisions about how I behave politically," Schulman says. "Lesbians are involved in every progressive movement for change on the face of the earth. And they don't demand the level of reciprocity in those other movements that they do in the gay movement.

"If I made my political decisions based on who I was going to have an equal relationship with, as a lesbian, I wouldn't be able to work with anyone. So instead, I make decisions based on my own morality and my own political views. There are plenty of men in ACT UP whom I find intolerable, yet somehow I can tolerate them in that context. Because basically we are in agreement in terms of the broader spectrum.

"I've also been frustrated by the inability of lesbians to coalesce politically. If there were a vibrant, activist lesbian movement going on, I'm sure I would want to be part of it, but there isn't. [Schulman has since joined the group Lesbian Avengers, which was founded in September 1992.] My own political belief system determines that I have to be involved where people are organizing. I didn't come to ACT UP because the men like me or don't like me; I'm there because I have certain beliefs."

Schulman's beliefs also have led her to speak out publicly about the controversy engendered during the early 1990s when the National Endowment for the Arts (NEA), pressured by right-wing fundamentalists, repeatedly rescinded or denied grants to allegedly "obscene" artists, many of whom were gay. But while the progressive gay and lesbian community spoke out against this politically motivated censorship, Schulman's protest was unusual in that it focused on her gay and lesbian peers in the arts community as well as on conservatives and the NEA. She addressed race and class issues, and the fact that it traditionally has been white, middle-class artists who have benefited from arts awards.

"[At first], I was the *only* person saying [those things]," Schulman asserts. "And I came under incredible personal pressure to not do that. The whole process was very frightening for me, because I knew that I was isolating myself from people, and I was interfering with people's money, which is really the issue here.

"I recently debated Jennie Livingston [the white director of the documentary *Paris Is Burning*, about poor, young gay men of color and their cross-dressing 'vogue' dance parties] at a benefit," Schulman continues. "I was arguing that what's evolving is this sphere of *official gay culture*, which is gay and lesbian artwork that is promoted and [made a commodity] in the mainstream. The community has to ask if this work is being propelled because it resonates with and represents gay people, or if it is the product of a small sector who, for reasons of class and race, can position themselves strategically.

"Jennie was essentially arguing that if you just work really hard, you can get ahead. And it was interesting, because the audience *really* wanted to believe her. Because her message was that yes, we will be accepted, we will be seen as normal. And my message is, no, we are not normal, we will always be marginalized, and we make a terrible mistake if we buy into this kind of tokenism. I could see people struggling emotionally, but they really couldn't break with the hope of being accepted."

Sarah Schulman may or may not need acceptance of her viewpoint or her work; most artists do, on some level. And few of us are willing to risk losing that acceptance by speaking our consciences when our viewpoint is unpopular. Schulman's tenacious honesty ultimately may be as valuable a contribution to our community as her spirited novels.

Schulman vs. *Rent*

Achy Obejas / 1997

From the *Chicago Tribune*, November 10, 1997. © 1997 the *Chicago Tribune*.
All rights reserved. Distributed by Tribune Content Agency, LLC.

Here's the story: A self-involved East Village performance artist dumps her male lover for a lesbian social activist, leaving the guy in a funk, and creates a performance piece that targets an avaricious landlord and causes a riot. All around them, people are dying of AIDS and neglect. Their best buds, a gay male couple in which one of the guys is HIV positive, is eventually consumed by the disease. His death adds new meaning to the lives of the survivors, who are redeemed by love.

Sounds like *Rent*, Jonathan Larson's multimillion-dollar Broadway smash that opens in Chicago on Tuesday night, right?

Except that it's *People in Trouble*, a 1984 novel about AIDS and activism penned by Sarah Schulman, a New York fiction writer. Schulman is convinced that Larson, now dead, pirated her novel in the creation of *Rent*.

While she's talking to lawyers about filing suit (she's not yet done so), Schulman has written a book about what she claims is Larson's plagiarism, *Stagestruck: Theater, AIDS and the Marketing of Gay America*, coming out next year from Duke University Press. In it, Schulman claims that Larson, who died of a brain aneurysm on the night of *Rent*'s final dress rehearsal in 1996, couldn't have written the play without being familiar with her work.

Schulman says Larson employed her storyline, characters and even certain details such as the watch alarms used by people with AIDS in the early and mid-1980s to remind them to take their medication. "He ripped me off," she says.

At least one person—Michael Korie, an opera librettist who worked with Schulman on a stage treatment of *People in Trouble*—claims Larson told him in 1994 that he read Schulman's book while he was developing *Rent*.

"We were at an awards presentation and we were both seated at the same table," says Korie. "To the best of my recollection, he described (what he was working on) as a love triangle set in the Lower East Side of Manhattan in the lives of people who were grappling with issues of AIDS, arts and homelessness; he described it as a *La bohème* for the nineties."

But to Korie, Larson had just described Schulman's novel. "I asked Jonathan Larson, 'Did you ever hear of *People in Trouble*?' and he responded with surprise and said, 'It's funny you should mention that—I didn't think too many people were familiar with it.' He said it had influenced his ideas on his own show. I don't remember the exact words. At the time, I didn't think anything of it."

Although Korie believes Larson used Schulman's book—or possibly the treatment of *People in Trouble* that made the rounds of New York theaters in the late 1980s—he doesn't attribute the similarities to deliberate plagiarism.

"Sometimes ideas get in the air," he says. "I admire Jonathan's work, and I also admire Sarah's. This is just a terribly unfortunate situation."

The attorneys for Larson's family and estate dismiss all of Schulman's allegations. "I've never heard of Sarah Schulman and I've never heard of Jonathan being familiar with her book," says Orin Snyder, a lawyer and spokesperson for the Larson family. "No one has copyright over AIDS, the East Village, homosexuality, performance art or watch alarms."

Both *Rent* and *People in Trouble* share the same milieu: an apocalyptic New York in which artists and poor people, at the mercy of ever-more-greedy real estate developers, are being driven out of their homes. Both Larson's and Schulman's characters are surrounded by homeless street vendors and junkies, and are in constant danger of having nowhere to go.

In both the show and the novel, there's a heterosexual coupling that's ruptured when the woman artist has an affair with a lesbian social activist. Also in both works, the male lover and the lesbian interloper meet by accident and end up liking each other and chatting about their common lover.

In the novel, Molly, the lesbian, and Kate, the artist, become involved with an AIDS activist group that targets a greedy landlord trying to evict poor people, artists and people with AIDS. In *Rent*, the group of friends, including Joanne, the lawyer, and Maureen, the artist, organize against a landlord who's trying to evict poor people, artists, and people with AIDS.

In *People in Trouble*, Molly and Kate attend to a gay male activist friend as he lies dying from AIDS, which inspires them to fight for their beliefs—including the right of people to food and shelter. In *Rent*, a friend's death from AIDS—attended by Maureen and Joanne, among others—confirms the group's belief in love.

In the novel, Kate creates a performance piece—an installation goes up in flames—which causes a full-scale riot. In *Rent*, Maureen creates a performance piece—the audience ends up mooing en masse—which also leads to a riot. The outcomes, however, are different: In Schulman's story, the landlord is killed during the riot. In *Rent*'s sunnier version, the landlord repents.

Most of the similarities with Schulman's novel lie within the first act of *Rent*. The second act, which is much shorter, more closely parallels Giacomo Puccini's opera *La bohème*, which Larson acknowledged as inspiration from the start (and which coincidentally just opened over the weekend at the Lyric Opera, even as the Chicago road company is in previews for *Rent*). *La bohème*, which premiered in 1895 in Italy, depicts artists, composers and their friends leading a life of romanticized poverty. The biggest difference between Puccini's opera and Larson's musical is that *La bohème*'s Mimi dies, and *Rent*'s Mimi does not.

In *People in Trouble*, the action is seen through the eyes of Molly, the lesbian protagonist. In *Rent*, the story is told through Mark, Maureen's heterosexual filmmaker boyfriend who mostly stands back and watches. (In fact, at one point, he's chastised for his passivity by his best buddy, Roger.)

By changing the point of view of the story, Schulman asserts, Larson also subtly transformed the meaning of the story. "Now—in *Rent*—straight people are the heroes of the AIDS crisis, which is just not true," says Schulman, who was a member of ACT UP, the AIDS activist group, for seven years. "In *Rent*, straight people never have to deal with the guilt of having abandoned gay people during the AIDS crisis."

There are other specific points of commonality in the two works beyond the story line. In *People in Trouble*, an AIDS activist group steals credit card numbers to feed the poor. In *Rent*, Tom, a gay man, uses an ATM machine for similar purposes. In both, watch alarms play a symbolic role in alerting people with AIDS to take their medicines on time.

But while watch alarms were common in the mid-1980s, when Schulman was writing *People in Trouble*, they were passe by 1991, when Larson began concentrating in earnest on *Rent*. In the mid-1980s, AZT was being dispensed in four-hour intervals, but by 1991 AZT was being prescribed in twelve-hour cycles, thus eliminating the need for alarms.

"The idea of the watch alarms—the whole scene—comes straight out of *People in Trouble*," asserts Schulman.

Still, proving plagiarism is a rough road. "The problem is you can't copyright an idea," explains Burton Joseph, a media lawyer who has represented Playboy Enterprises, among other clients, in 1st Amendment and copyright cases. "What you have a proprietary interest in is the completed work. What you'd have to show is not that the idea was lifted from the book but rather that the words, the construction, the format, was copied from the book."

Schulman, however, is not the only one out there who says that Larson is using her material. Lynn M. Thomson, credited as the show's dramaturge, filed a $40 million lawsuit against Larson's estate demanding coauthorship and a percentage of the profits. In court papers, Thomson said she wrote 9 percent of the song lyrics and 48 percent of the recitative-style libretto.

Though the judge acknowledged Thomson's considerable contributions to the final script of *Rent*, Thomson lost the case last July. The judge ruled on a strict interpretation of intent—according to the law, coauthorship requires a mutual agreement of co-ownership of material, and in his opinion, there was no compelling evidence that Larson ever intended to extend such a right to Thomson. Thomson has since filed an appeal, and a decision is expected later this month.

When Schulman wrote *People in Trouble*, she had high hopes for it both as a book and as a stage project. In fact, she withheld theatrical rights from Dutton, its publisher, because she had entered into a prepublication agreement with Korie for the stage treatment.

But there were no takers on the stage production. Although the book received critical praise, including a review in the *New York Times* that called it "a strong, nervy and challenging novel," *People in Trouble* sold a modest five thousand hardcover copies and about fifteen thousand in paperback. It was translated into three languages and optioned for a film treatment.

Schulman didn't hear about Larson or *Rent* until 1996, when she went to review the show as a critic for the *New York Press*, a cultural newsweekly. But, amazingly, Schulman didn't see the similarities with her own work until it was pointed out to her by a friend.

Professionally, it was a precarious time for Schulman: Her longtime agent, Diane Cleaver, had just died and her file had been passed on to a junior agent who wasn't familiar or interested in her work. At Dutton, her books were steady backlist sellers, but the publishing industry was going through its own convulsions and authors like Schulman, whose works (*Rat Bohemia*, *My American History*, *After Delores* and others) got good reviews but fell short on sales, had fallen out of favor.

When Schulman notified Carole DeSanti, her longtime editor at Dutton, DeSanti reminded her that Schulman herself had retained theatrical rights to *People in Trouble*.

Shortly after Schulman made her claims against *Rent*, Dutton released her from her option after four books and ten years. She believes the two events are related, that Dutton simply didn't want a troublesome writer on its roster.

DeSanti disagrees. "She wanted to go elsewhere, she was very unhappy, so I released her from her option. I can't say she asked to be released in so many words, but it was clear to both of us that it was time for a change for her."

Just about then, a short piece ran in *New York* magazine about Schulman's allegations. Some of the grassroots gay and lesbian press, including Chicago's *Outlines*, ran the story as well. But when Schulman turned to the national lesbian and gay news magazines, they passed on the story.

Judy Wieder, editor-in-chief of *The Advocate*, where Schulman is listed as a contributor, says the publication was waiting for a lawsuit on which to peg an article. It would be the same reason given Schulman by all the nongay media outlets she contacted as well.

"That's when I decided to just write a book about it," she says. "The truth is, I just can't function on the level of the power of *Rent*. It's worth millions. [David] Geffen owns the music. [Robert] De Niro owns the film rights. So I wrote my book, I have had my say with it, and I hope it'll make people look at *People in Trouble* as an authentic record of the AIDS crisis, not commodified, mainstream work like *Rent*. "

When Larson first started work on *Rent* with Billy Aronson, who is still credited with the original concept for the show, none of the elements it has in common with *People in Trouble* were in place.

"I had an idea to update *La bohème*," says Aronson, who receives royalties from *Rent*. "But from the beginning, Jonathan and I had different ideas."

According to Aronson, Larson wanted the piece to be about AIDS. His best friend from high school was HIV positive and Larson had been accompanying him to a support group.

So Larson and Aronson parted. At that time, Larson was a struggling composer and playwright with few credits to his name—among them, *Superbia*, which he had staged at Playwrights Horizons, and his one-person show, *Tick, Tick . . . BOOM!* Additionally, Larson had done some work for *Sesame Street* and film scores for Steven Spielberg's video-cassette children's projects.

Though he was known in New York theater as an inventive and original composer, Larson's reputation for storytelling was lacking. In fact, when he first brought *Rent* to New York Theater Workshop, he was advised to hire a librettist to write the book for the musical. Even after *Rent* was well into production, the play's narrative was in constant peril. That's why Thomson, the dramaturge, was brought in.

"When I got it, it had no coherent structure," she says. "Jonathan was a genius as a composer but he had a lot of limitations as a playwright."

In fact, the official *Rent* book freely acknowledges that Thomson had a major hand in shaping *Rent*; the judge in her case also recognized that Larson had problems with the show's story line until Thomson came along.

By the time Thomson was on board, however, most of the similarities with *People in Trouble* were evident. But Thomson says Larson never mentioned Schulman or the book as a source.

"We discussed impulses and origins of what he'd created so far and it had nothing to do with Sarah's book," says Thomson. "It was *La bohème* and his friends."

Ironically, Thomson takes great exception to Schulman's characterization of Larson's work as derivative or opportunistic. "He had such love for his friends who were gay," she says. "He wanted to honor them with *Rent*."

And at least some gay people agree. "I thought *Rent* was excellent, incredibly moving," says Sarah Petit, executive editor of *Out* magazine. "The gay characters in *Rent* are, by and large, there to be liked by a broad audience. It's not as far as we want to be, but it's further than we've been."

But Petit doesn't easily dismiss Schulman either. "There are certainly similarities there, and Sarah raises interesting points—where is the line between artistic influence and wholesale ripoff? What constitutes influence and what constitutes inappropriate appropriation?"

Those, of course, are Schulman's own questions.

Man in the Hot Seat

Sarah Schulman and Andrew Sullivan / 1999

From *The Advocate*, January 19, 1999. Reprinted with permission of EqualPride.

In gay and lesbian publishing this year, Andrew Sullivan scored a win with his book *Love Undetectable: Notes on Friendship, Sex, and Survival* (Knopf). Sarah Schulman won kudos as well with *Shimmer* (Avon) and *Stagestruck* (Duke University Press). In hopes of a lively exchange, *The Advocate* put these two leading lights of the gay movement together. The following highlights from their dialogue provide a snapshot of the deep convictions and rifts that make up the contemporary gay and lesbian landscape in America.

Sarah Schulman: You say in your book, talking about promiscuity: "I feel unable to live up to the ideals that I really hold." What makes it so hard?

Andrew Sullivan: I'm saying I have never gone on my high horse and started judging people for their sexual expression. The book tries to get away from discussing sex to discussing what sex really means—its relationship to intimacy and love and commitment—and why we need to bring ourselves into a place where love is more the center of our lives rather than mere sexuality.

SS: What is the contradiction within the lived experience that is so hard?

AS: We have a lot of internalized problems of self-esteem in that we've been taught not to believe that we're worthy of love.

SS: Are you saying that people who have sex outside of love are operating from a place of low self-esteem?

AS: Yes. I think they often are.

SS: People who describe themselves as sex radicals advocate for practices you're describing as partially motivated by low self-esteem. Do you feel they're missing an insight?

AS: Yes. But this is not what my book is about. I think even [sex radicals] would argue that some people's compulsive sexual activities and inability to construct emotional relationships around sex are not purely some act of political choice. They are complicated emotional situations, and most people would rather they weren't in them.

SS: Is having sex only in the context of relationships a sign of more emotional health?

AS: To find a committed way to integrate sex and love is wonderful. Virtually everybody acknowledges that. But it isn't the only model. In the book I'm very careful to talk about friendship as the model of love that is profound and important.

Even in your questioning—sex is a part of it, obviously, but to place it at the center of the book is really not about the book. It's about a particular attempt to define gay people by sex. That is precisely what the book challenges.

SS: You're saying that if people could fully realize their capacity for love, they would not be engaging in what is currently gay male sexual culture outside of relationships.

AS: "Gay male sexual culture outside of relationships" is a very broad description.

SS: In your work you describe Catholicism in compelling homoerotic terms. Do you feel that the human-Jesus relationship is as erotic for women within Catholicism?

AS: I think it can be. Ask Camille Paglia. [*Laughs*] The wonderful thing about Catholicism is that in the figure of Mary, the iconography of the female is also deeply embedded in Catholic teaching. And even the idea that the church itself is the bride of Christ.

SS: Women have had horrible struggles within the Catholic Church. Do you see this as a contradiction?

AS: No, just as gay men have had an awful time. I'm in favor of women priests and always have been. But I think one can live in the faith while accepting the church as an institution that has done and still does terrible things.

SS: You write about the ex-gay movement. Is [the movement] a fundamentalist strategy to recruit gay people to the religious right?

AS: [*Laughs*] If it were, [gay people] are a little smarter than that. I think the people who are going to be "recruited" are very few and very conflicted.

SS: Why are they putting so much money into it?

AS: They are desperately trying to chip away at the notion that homosexuality is unchosen because once most people accept it as involuntary, their broader political argument is so much weaker. Politically, their strategy is aimed at heterosexuals, not gay people.

SS: The biological determinism argument is mostly embraced by gay men. Lesbians have a long history of arguing for their sexuality as a choice.

AS: In fact, most of them don't.

SS: In 1980 there was a famous article by Adrienne Rich on "the lesbian continuum." Lesbians can conceptualize their sexuality on a continuum in relationship to men, male power, and women. I'm not saying women oppose biological determinism, but I think emotionally they understand their sexuality in a different way.

AS: I do too. That's part of what I think are enormous differences between lesbian sexuality and gay male sexuality.

SS: Are those differences biological?

AS: Yes, partly. It is much easier for women to attach sexual attraction to a prior emotional attraction, whereas men tend to have a sexual attraction and then have to graft emotional feelings onto that.

SS: Gabriel Rotello wrote about the lesbian relationship as an ideal, something for gay men to aspire to. A lot of women responded to him negatively, not wanting to be seen as a domesticating model that gay men should be compared to. Are you aware of that debate?

AS: [*Laughs*] There are debates that take place within a few blocks of lower Manhattan, and then there are debates that actually take place.

SS: This was in the pages of *The Nation*.

AS: Oh, well, I'd stick by the few blocks of lower Manhattan. No one is saying that people have to be this way but that there are certain radical differences between gay male culture and lesbian culture.

SS: But you're arguing they are biological.

AS: The evidence is overwhelming that they are partly biological and partly cultural. I think sexual attraction is more visceral with men than with women. That goes for straight as well as gay men. And women tend to be more able to integrate their emotional and sexual lives. It has to do with levels of testosterone and estrogen and with evolutionary psychology.

SS: So you're really rejecting the thirty-year argument of the feminist movement that biology is not destiny.

AS: I never say in the book or anywhere that biology is destiny. I say that it is simply part of what makes one who one is, and ignoring that will lead you to all sorts of frustrations and an inability to understand what is going on.

SS: Do you believe that life begins at conception?

AS: Where in the book does that come up? It's like you have a list of PC questions.

SS: You're very clear about your relationship to the Catholic faith. That's front and center in your presentation to the public.

AS: Since I don't talk about that in the book, why is it relevant?

SS: You are a spokesperson for the gay and lesbian community. You are one of the few in the community who has access to the mainstream media.

AS: So do you.

SS: No, I don't.

AS: So does anyone who wants to write.

SS: So do you want to pass?

AS: No, I'll answer your question. Yes, I do think that at a fundamental level, life does begin at conception.

SS: Are you in favor of a repeal of *Roe v. Wade*?

AS: Yes. But I'm not in favor of making abortion illegal tomorrow or of a constitutional amendment to make it illegal. I have taken a very strong stance on prolife terrorism. There is such a deep division of moral belief in our culture that I would not make it illegal for someone to have an abortion in the first trimester, ever. I still think it's wrong and could not myself be a party to it, but I would defend the right of someone to go ahead.

SS: Are you involved in grassroots organizing on the marriage issue?

AS: Have I gone to cities and talked and raised money about it? Yes.

SS: But have you ever been involved in a community-based grassroots organization? I was in ACT UP for seven years. I know you weren't.

AS: I'm not a group person. I never have been. I've worked closely with Lambda [Legal Defense and Education Fund]. I've done events for them, gone around the country for the [Gay and Lesbian] Victory Fund, raised money speaking for the Human Rights Campaign.

SS: You are the most visible gay person in the media of this country. You're on the most prime-time talk shows; you're in the *New York Times*. Are you surprised that you have become the token fag, I guess, the token gay man represented in the media?

AS: [*Laughs*] All I've ever done is defend my writing, and if I'm asked to go on TV, I've gone on. I think you can either talk to a mainstream audience or you can't. Obviously they think I can, so they ask me back. But it's not a question of access. It is really up to them.

SS: But I think you see yourself as representing a minority opinion within the gay community.

AS: No, I don't. The vast majority agree with much of what I say. Only a very small minority of people feel threatened by certain arguments and ideas.

SS: And how do you assess that?

AS: Once upon a time, when the gay world was smaller, it was more easily controlled by a particular political faction. It has become more diverse, and the old elites are very threatened. So they attempt to demonize or stigmatize or marginalize people they disagree with.

SS: OK, that's your scenario. Let me offer you mine. I think quite a few people have come from the grass roots up and built a community. They have a great deal of legitimacy within that community. But they have never been recognized by the dominant culture. They have never been offered a voice at the highest level. They are watching people be selected whose views are most acceptable to the dominant group.

AS: You really think arguing for same-sex marriage is most acceptable? I think it is the one argument most likely to provoke opposition.

SS: I recall that before the AIDS crisis, gay marriage was considered preposterous, but once there was ACT UP doing things like going into Saint Patrick's Cathedral—

AS: You think that made same-sex marriage more palatable.

SS: Yes, absolutely.

AS: [*Laughs*] I think it's ludicrous. AIDS brought gay and straight America into a dialogue, and because it reasserted the notion among many gay people of our equality and dignity, marriage came to the fore naturally. I'm not telling straight America what it wants to hear. It doesn't want to hear that we demand marriage rights or that we deserve to be equal in the military.

SS: But I think that position is more palatable than a defense of a community-based culture and a rejection of privatized family units on a reproductive model. That's what they don't want to hear.

AS: That's what they love to hear. There is nothing the mainstream likes more than some person standing up and saying, "We gay people reject all that you stand for." That keeps us where we belong as far as they're concerned.

SS: My lesbian friends are having children now, and suddenly their families who rejected them for twenty years are welcoming them back because they fit some model of motherhood.

AS: You want to stop them doing that?

SS: No.

AS: So what's your issue?

SS: You said they reject our wanting to enter society on their terms. But I say no, the more we resemble their ideas of how we should behave—

AS: It's a human model. It is not a heterosexual monopoly. To define ourselves by where we've been instead of where we're going is demeaning, I'm not out there to win a popularity contest. Even if you despise everything I've ever written, you can't say I've sought out popularity.

SS: I think you're not a leader who has emerged from the community; I think you've been selected by the dominant group.

AS: I haven't been selected by anybody. All I've done is write and think and go out there.

SS: But other people do that too, and they don't have the same access. You know that, right?

AS: I don't know that. I think anybody can have access. I didn't come with any particular privilege. I don't understand what that means. Anybody who can speak and write coherently can have access, period.

You keep referring to extreme leftists as the community. They represent a tiny fraction of gay people in this country. We know from exit polls that 33 percent of gay people voted Republican in 1998. Are they not the community? Where do they come from? They are the people being marginalized by the old gay elites who want to keep their power.

SS: What power?

AS: The power to define who is gay or not.

SS: All those people did was give their lives to building a movement that made it possible for people like you to come out.

AS: Nonsense. I came out because I came out.

SS: No, a social context was created in which you could come out.

AS: Believe me, I should be able to talk about why I came out. The existence of an extreme left wing as the representation of gay people prevented me from coming out. It prevents other people from coming out, because if they have to be "queer," they're not going to come out. The establishment of these left-wing elites actually impedes the possibility of gay people's living fulfilled lives. It keeps them back in the ghettos.

SS: Come on, you know the people who make change are not the people who benefit from it. The drag queens who started Stonewall twenty-something years ago are no better off now than they were then.

AS: That's ridiculous. Of course they're better off. And I would defend drag queens—as I do in my book—to the nth degree.

SS: Well, that's the vanguard that started the gay movement.

AS: It is not. You need to go back a few decades, and you'll see people who didn't look at all like drag queens. In the leftist view of the world, the

Mattachine Society didn't exist. In my view the gay movement was hijacked in the seventies.

SS: By street activists.

AS: Yes.

SS: So in your view Stonewall was the downfall of the gay movement.

AS: Yes. It was a diversion from our capacity to integrate into society.

SS: Exactly how do you think change does get made?

AS: It gets made every time a human being stands up for a principle that makes sense to him.

Behind *Enemies*' Lines

Dan Bacalzo / 2007

From *TheaterMania*, February 7, 2007. Reprinted with permission of the author.

When she was six years old, Sarah Schulman received a copy of *The Diary of Anne Frank* from her grandmother. "The lesson I learned from reading it is that girls can be writers," says Schulman. "I started a diary and wrote in it, 'When I grow up, I will write books.'" She's kept that childhood promise, with novels such as *Empathy*, *People in Trouble*, and the soon-to-be-released *The Child*.

Schulman is also author of more than a dozen plays, including *Carson McCullers* and *Manic Flight Reaction*. Her latest project is an adaptation of the Isaac Bashevis Singer novel *Enemies, A Love Story*, which makes its world premiere this month at the Wilma Theater in Philadelphia. The playwright will be on hand after the Thursday, February 15, performance for an audience talkback.

Like the novel, the play is set in 1949 and centers around Herman, a Jewish survivor of the Holocaust who marries the German woman who saved him, later finds his first wife is still alive, and then, incredibly, weds a third woman.

TheaterMania: How did you begin your playwriting career?
Sarah Schulman: I had my first play produced in 1979 at 2 a.m. at the Pyramid Club on Avenue A. I was deeply involved in the downtown arts community—I guess you could call what I did performance art. There were scripts, but I worked with improvisation people and choreographers. 1994 was my last downtown production. I had a show at PS122 that I really loved, and moved it to HERE, which had just opened. They had no air conditioner, and it was the middle of the summer. It was so hot, the actors thought they were going to pass out. We opened up part of the theater to let the air in and the lot next door was filled with rats. So the director and I were standing at the door with sticks trying to keep the rats out of the theater. He turned to

me, and said, "Isn't this glamorous?" And I thought, "I don't want to do this anymore. Enough is enough."

TM: So, then what did you do?

SS: I had to either give up or become an uptown playwright. That took a lot out of me, because I had to learn to write in a completely different way. The innovations of the avant-garde in the last 150 years have not made it into uptown theater. They're still into conventional narrative structure, and "whose play is this?" and "drama is change" and all that stuff that the rest of us know is no longer true. But you can't argue with them. At first I tried to discuss it, but it's not discussable. So I just had to learn how to do it. It took me until 2002—eight years—to actually get in, to cross 14th Street. The way it happened was, I was at OutWrite, which used to be the gay writers' conference; it doesn't exist anymore. Craig Lucas was on a panel, and I said something from on the floor, and he got hysterical and started screaming at me.

TM: What did you say?

SS: They were talking about Jesse Helms, and I said there was censorship within the theater community and not just from Jesse Helms. There were power structures that excluded certain people from theater and you didn't need the Republicans to enforce them. And he screamed at me. A few weeks later, I got a phone call from him and he apologized and took me out to dinner. We had a great talk and I told him I was writing a play, and he asked to read it. At that time, he had decided he wanted to become a director. So we started a two-year process of trying to get a production of this play, in which we had reading after reading at the Public, the Vineyard, you name it. It didn't get produced, but it got me into the "uptown playwright" circles.

TM: What was your first exposure to *Enemies*?

SS: I saw the movie version in '89, when it first came out, and it spoke to me because my grandmother had two sisters who were killed in the Holocaust. Even though I had no direct survivors in my immediate group, my family was very impacted. I grew up in New York with a lot of kids who were children of Holocaust survivors. My first girlfriend was a child of Jewish refugees. There were a lot of things in the movie that were familiar to me, such as the way people were yelling at each other, and angry at each other, even though they weren't hurting each other. The pain was caused by somebody else. It's about the emotional consequences of trauma.

TM: That's a theme in several of your works.

SS: I've been frustrated because a lot of what I've written about AIDS or gay and lesbian characters has been very hard to get produced. In a way,

I'm using this play as code. I began to realize that when you have a group of people who are despised, like gay people, or Jewish people, or Black people, and then they have an extraordinary trauma on top of the usual trauma, the way the dominant culture can deal with representing it is to make them noble, pure, clean, and innocent. So the fact that something bad happens to them is really sad. In that way, you end up with these desexualized gay male characters who are not angry and not in any political movement, and are abandoned and then you feel empathy for them. These types of stories are based on a Christian paradigm that suffering makes you better. But actually, suffering makes you worse. People who were victimized were real people before their victimization. They were complex, some of them were nasty or did bad things. They were filled with contradictions.

TM: In Singer's novel, Herman wasn't exactly a great husband even before the war.

SS: That's one of the things about the material that appealed to me. To show people in all of their flaws before the trauma, does that mean you have less sympathy for their trauma?

TM: What changes did you make in your adaptation?

SS: It took me four years to convince the Singer estate to let me have the rights. But once they did, they've been incredibly supportive in allowing me to make very dramatic changes. Since I'm a novelist and a playwright, I understand that each form takes a different impulse. Plays are what people say and do, while novels are really about interiority, about what people remember, see, and feel. Singer is almost like a magical realist; he believes in the other world, and the other world and this world are constantly interacting. He's very abstract in his images. It's not a conventional narrative structure, and it doesn't drive forward in a conventional narrative way. So, that was one issue. The other issue was that I had a lot of questions about the female representation in the novel.

TM: Given your previous work, I had wondered about that.

SS: I let all the women have complexity and agency. By making the female characters Herman's equals in terms of their desires for themselves and their own lives, it enables them to engage him in active dialogue. They're looking for an answer for their pain and trying to imagine a better life. So, the thoughts that used to all belong to Herman in the novel are now spread out and expressed actively in their relationships. It's really like a different story, yet it engages all the same themes, but for a contemporary audience. Women are alienated enough going to the theater. I want them to see something that will wake them up, emotionally.

TM: How do you think audiences familiar with the novel or movie are going to react to the changes?

SS: I think they're going to love it. It's really funny, and it's very Judaic, very dialogic. It's got that kind of philosophical profundity that's very entertaining. I've always tried to be funny, to look at dark things from the insider's point of view. As Brecht said, when you see the man crying on stage, you want the audience to laugh; when you see him laughing, you want the audience to cry. This material really enables that kind of audience response.

TM: What appeals to you about the process of adaptation?

SS: As an intellectual, I have had to learn that I can't just cut out the greatest works of Western civilization because they're so prejudiced. You have to look for the brilliance of certain human themes and then extend them to include ourselves. That's the challenge and interesting thing about writing adaptations, and it works for me. As soon as I realized that I had to take those themes and expand them to the specificity of other human beings' daily lives, I got very excited by the whole process. It's like opening up the world of literature and the world of ideas to include the rest of us.

Sarah Schulman's *The Child*: The Toxic Machine

Ernest Hardy / 2007

From *LA Weekly*, July 11, 2007. Reprinted with permission.

In 1997, fifteen-year-old Sam Manzie sexually assaulted and murdered eleven-year-old Eddie Werner. Those are the bare facts. Shrouding them, however, are complex, interlocked issues: queer teen sexuality, pedophilia, homophobia in macro and micro forms, and the explicit and insidious ways that the state, mainstream culture and families can converge to drive queer folk mad—and then blame the victim for the fallout. Novelist and playwright Sarah Schulman's eleventh book, *The Child*, is based on the Manzie case. It examines the dynamic of cause and effect between sanctioned manifestations of homophobia and the consequential alienation and madness (low-flame or combusted) still suffered by many gays and lesbians. As she writes of one of the novel's lesbian characters, "First, they humiliated her for being gay, so she became isolated. Sequence, consequence."

Manzie's sexual relationship with Stephen Simmons, whom the boy met online when he was fourteen and Simmons was forty-three, was cited by the teen's family and by the court as the trigger behind the murder. Manzie had been corrupted.

Schulman uses that tragedy as the foundation for *The Child*. In her quest to make sense of damaged queer psyches, she sifts through recent political and cultural history. She makes note of how the American legal system enforces not only law, but homophobic Judeo-Christian morality, and outlines ways that the American health care industry specifically fails women and gay men. At its core, though, the book is a painful but astute observation of the roles played by families themselves in inflicting spiritual wounds. The main players are Eva, a Jewish lawyer born in the sixties but shaped by the New York of the seventies, and her California-born and -raised gentile girlfriend, a frustrated playwright; Hockey, a gay lawyer battling HIV; and fifteen-year-old Stew, whose slow descent into insanity makes for wrenching reading. In true Schulman form, the book has a gleaming intelligence and chilled anger. It's beautifully blunt and plainspoken. Schulman recently spoke with the *Weekly* by phone from her home in New York.

LA Weekly: In the afterword for *The Child*, you write, "The novel you hold in your hand was ready for publication in 1999. It reflects a world of perceptions and values firmly grounded in that year." And you express regret that neither you nor the reader was able to experience the book in the moment in which it was meant to be read. Can you explain or define that specific moment and how it led to *The Child* being written?

Sarah Schulman: It was finished in '99. That's the moment where protease inhibitors were beginning to be widely used, but they still had enormous toxic side effects. People who had expected to die were instead plummeted into this kind of merry-go-round of extreme drug reactions and dramatic ups and downs. It looked like things were going to change but at a very high price. So, there's a great deal of emotional change and uncertainty, and physical discomfort. Also technologically, it's when people are starting to get cell phones and to really be online, but most people are still waiting at phone booths and carrying quarters around in their pockets. So culturally, it's quite different. Stew is young, so he is living online, but that's very mysterious to older people.

I also think at that time there was still a common outrage and recognition of how the marginalization was hurting people. I feel that now people are so assaulted and beaten down by being lied to culturally for so long that there's not even a place to articulate those kinds of feelings. I think the book looks so unusual today, but had it been published in its time, it would have been more in sync with how people were looking at things. I don't think there's anything like it being published now, because I don't think we're as aware now. I think we're much more blunted. The culture is moving backward.

LAW: You say the novel was finished in '99. When did you start it? What took so long for it to get published?

SS: It took my friend Diamanda Galás picking up a phone and making it happen. No one wanted to touch it, and I think it's because I wasn't condemning the relationship between Stew and the older men. When I got to Carroll & Graf, my editor and I were very far apart culturally, and he had a very hard time understanding the book. So, there are three or four extremely explanatory paragraphs that I don't really like, but I was forced to put them in to help him understand what the book was doing.

LAW: What was it about the Manzie case that attracted you?

SS: He was a young man, about fifteen, who lived in New Jersey and who had gone online looking for an older man to have sex with. The [older] guy got caught in a pedophilia Internet sting, and the kid got exposed to his community. At that point, [Manzie] had a psychotic episode and murdered a little boy. When he chose his own boyfriend, they said he was a child. But when he killed somebody, he was tried as an adult. They offered him a deal where if he would say that he was molested, he could plea bargain. He refused and took a thirty-year sentence, which he is now serving. That case profoundly affected me, and so I think I started with that story. . . . You know, each character at a different point in the story is the child. It's really about the consequences of familial homophobia on people's emotional lives, that it has a very, very wide range of consequence that each of the characters experiences in their own way, but it's dramatically determining in how their lives unfold.

LAW: That aspect of the book—the stark truthfulness of the simple observation that society and family really do drive so many gays and lesbians mad, and then the victim is blamed for the madness and the consequences of it—is . . .

SS: . . . the classic American structure of oppression. You have a systemic oppression that is invisible and looks normal, and then people become pathologized because of its consequences on their lives.

LAW: At one point, you write, "The struggle to love justice was so hard in this era; the barriers so intense." Where do you find hope?

SS: Well, you know, I am very optimistic, as you can see by looking at the effort that I make. I make a huge effort to create work and to bring it into the world and to talk about it intelligently with people I know I can have a real conversation with. Right now, because public life is so untrue and so little that is said in public is true, the thing that I rely on [is] other individuals who I know are committed to being accountable. I rely on being in dialogue with them. That's the holding pattern until the Zeitgeist changes. I mean, it was Diamanda Galás who got my book published—it wasn't Edmund White. [*Laughs*] The people who are on the margins, who know what's real, can actually help each other, even if we don't control representation.

LAW: The trick is finding those people on the margins who are not just using their outsider status as a way to secure a place for themselves in the machine. Quite often, the ones who are lifted up are those who will maintain things just as they are.

SS: Yes, that is true for the most part. And sometimes there are people who get caught up in it who try to be conscious and try to maintain something articulate in what they're making, but that's very difficult. That's why you have to be part of a community. Otherwise, you're just an individual, and ultimately you become an opportunist, even against your better judgment. But if you're accountable to other people who don't have the power that you have, or at least if you're in dialogue with them on some level, there's a little more hope. It's a toxic machine, absolutely.

Monday Interview: Sarah Schulman

Dick Donahue / 2009

From *Publishers Weekly*, December 7, 2009. Copyright © PWxyz LLC, Publishers Weekly. All rights reserved.

Publishers Weekly: What would you like readers to take away from *Ties That Bind*?

Sarah Schulman: On the highest level, I would love readers to be inspired to rethink tired paradigms, and be encouraged by creative re-imaginings of how we can live with more awareness and accountability. We are in such a fascinating and complex time now, and many ideas that were censored during the cultural freeze of the Bush era may have a chance to be heard. I would love for people to be invigorated by new ideas, and to enjoy them.

PW: The subtitle of your new book is *Familial Homophobia and Its Consequences*. What are some of those consequences?

SS: My argument in brief is that the family is the place where most people, gay and straight, first learn about homophobia. And that the maintenance of gay people as lesser-than is subsequently enforced through the arts and entertainment industries and government policies, resulting in a diminishment of gay people's status and self-perception. I explain clearly, and with examples and arguments, that familial homophobia is not a personal problem, but is instead a cultural crisis. And that we can learn from the enormous paradigm shifts in how domestic violence is viewed, that abusive behavior inside families is a broad social concern and responsibility. Gay press reviews have been superb, and I recently had a standing room only reading in Chicago. The excitement and embracing of the book's ideas is very exciting. Ironically, of course, there has been a parallel blackout by the straight press. This interview is the very first engagement with a mainstream publication acknowledging that the book even exists. It's a strange through-the-looking-glass experience, one that I have had all my life. It speaks volumes that work that LGBT people love and embrace is often ignored completely by mainstream institutions.

PW: In what ways does familial homophobia differ from societal homophobia overall; is one or the other "form" more harmful?

SS: Now that most people know an openly gay person, I have come to realize that the word "society" is basically a euphemism for our families. It is in the family that people are often first rewarded for being straight and punished for being gay, even though there is nothing wrong with homosexuality and nothing right with heterosexuality. And this later gets played out in all of our social institutions.

PW: You've recently been awarded the prestigious Kessler Prize. Could you briefly describe that award, and its significance in your work?

SS: The Kessler is the highest honor in the gay world. It recognizes sustained contribution to LGBT studies; previous winners include Judith Butler, Samuel Delany, Edmund White, and Adrienne Rich. This recognition highlights that the community supports and praises my efforts to create complex sophisticated lesbian representation in novels, nonfiction and on stage, and my belief that this work can and will be integrated into mainstream American arts and ideas. These kinds of awards exist because of the exclusion of gay and especially lesbian artists from mainstream reward and recognition. I believe that all people can learn to universalize a lesbian protagonist in a book or play or film or TV program, and that this process has been stopped by fearful gatekeepers (producers, editors, agents, etc.) who preemptively keep this work from the public, by enforcing the "Bush doctrine" internally despite their private beliefs to the contrary. Being awarded the Kessler means that the LGBT community has had it with the exclusion of our authentic expression from center of the culture, and believes that lesbian writers should not have to eliminate or code lesbian protagonists in order to be appreciated for the quality of our contribution.

PW: You've written more novels than nonfiction books and plays. Is that your preferred category?

SS: Yes, I consider myself to be primarily a novelist. I do love to write plays, but the theater is far more conservative than the book business and the censorship is more pervasive. But I am a very, very optimistic person, and I believe that anything that humans create, humans can heal. Right now I am working on projects in all genres. I have a book coming next year from the University of California Press, *The Gentrification of the Mind: Witness to a Lost Imagination*, about the consequences of AIDS on housing and art production. I'm almost done with a new novel, *The Healing*, which is a remake of Balzac's *Cousin Bette* set in Greenwich Village in 1958. I recently had a reading of a new play, *The Lady Hamlet*, at the American Repertory Theater in Boston, and I'm waiting to hear its fate. Plus, my collaborator of twenty-four years, Jim Hubbard, and I continue to create the ACT UP Oral History Project (www.actuporalhistory.org), and I'm trying to figure out the best way to publish these interviews.

An Interview with Sarah Schulman

Carlos Motta / 2011

Interview conducted by Carlos Motta for his project *We Who Feel Differently*, January 17, 2011. Reprinted with permission.

We are constantly being told that things are so much better and we have made so much progress. I really think we have an enormous amount of change, but change is not the same thing as progress. The way gay people are contained, made secondary, and diminished is far more sophisticated now than it was twenty years ago ... Why are we being told this condition of profound oppression is actually progress? It is not.
—Sarah Schulman

Carlos Motta: I was researching your work and found a reading of "The Transformation of Silence into Language and Action," that you did for a conference on Audre Lorde for the University of Pennsylvania, and I wonder how this work, even its title, may represent a lot of the work you have done. Would you mind starting by talking about this text and Audre Lorde, or how these words resonate with your work?

Sarah Schulman: Audre Lorde was my professor at Hunter College and I learned many pedagogical tricks from her that have become important for the way I teach at a public university with large classes. I learned the importance of knowing every student's name and teaching from the center of the room. When you have a large class and they sit in rows you lose them, but when you have everyone in a circle with you in the center you are able to teach each student individually, to look them in the eye and say: "Remember when you said last week . . ." That is what she would do. She would also say things like: "Class, write this down . . . The message that you can't fight City Hall is a rumor being spread by City Hall!" The necessity to identify the dominant culture and people in power as responsible for the message that nothing changes and people cannot change anything was a very important education for me.

CM: What class was she teaching?

SS: This is hysterical. The class was called US Literature after World War II, the most banal class possible. At this time she recently had one breast removed and she did not wear any prosthesis. So she came in the first day, she had one breast and wore all this jewelry, and nobody in the class knew who she was because they were just taking an English requirement and she said: "Class, we are changing the name of this course to The Poet as Outsider." This was 1982 and she assigned the books *Understanding the New Black Poetry*, *Native American Poetry*, and *Lesbian Poetry*. As students we had to carry this book, *Lesbian Poetry*, on the subway and to class. I had never seen a teacher assign a book with a title like that ever in my life. In class, we would read the poems out loud and we were not allowed to discuss how the poem was written or what the poet was trying to say, we could only say how the poem made us feel.

What is interesting is that with rich and middle-class students you do not want to do that, as they are accustomed to talking about how they feel. Students in public universities however are not used to talking about how they feel, so this dialogue becomes an incredible teaching tool. One day she called on me to read a poem out loud; a Black poet from the 1960s, Don L. Lee, wrote it, and the poem had the word n----r in it about sixty times. So I am sitting there reading, "n----r, n----r, n----r, n----r," and she asks me: "What is the matter, Sarah?" and I reply that I feel uncomfortable saying this word and she asks me why, stating: "That word has no power for you, does it?" This is the kind of teacher she was, and now I like to use similar methods.

It is amazing that people mention Audre Lorde almost every day even though she has been dead for many years. There are very important cultural institutions named after her, including the Audre Lorde Project and the Callen-Lorde Center. Wherever you go in the world people mention her and are inspired by her. I teach her work now and always hand out "The Transformation of Silence into Language and Action." I tell my students Lorde was my teacher, and as we read and discuss, every student relates to this piece regardless of who they are. It is amazing. I have never seen a work that transcends all social categories as effectively.

CM: It is a text that seems to describe your activism, writing and teaching. What is an overview of your political work?

SS: As a writer, I have published sixteen books, including novels and nonfiction books. Each has gay, lesbian, or HIV-positive protagonists and people as its primary subject matter. As a playwright, I have produced plays with queer subject matter and am now writing movies featuring lesbian and queer protagonists. As an activist, I have participated in foundational political movements in this country. I started in the abortion rights movement because abortion only became legal in this country when I was fifteen. I then worked as an AIDS activist for almost thirty years. I founded The Lesbian Avengers and have been working for the last five years advocating for gay Irish people to be allowed to march in the St. Patrick's Day Parade in Manhattan, which still has not happened. I am currently organizing a US tour for leaders of the Palestinian queer movement. I cofounded MIX with Jim Hubbard, which is a lesbian and gay experimental film festival now twenty-four years old. We also founded the ACT UP Oral History Project, which is now ten years old. I have spent my life community building and insisting on the primacy and authority of marginalized people, putting them at the center of the story.

CM: What was your specific position with ACT UP and why is the formation and work of ACT UP such an important civil movement in the history of the United States? If we put this question in conversation with your memory of Audre Lorde, what strategies were being used to resist power during this time?

SS: I was a rank-and-file person in ACT UP. I was never part of its leadership, but I had been involved in direct-action politics before AIDS. There were people from a wide range of political experiences united by ACT UP. People came from the gay liberation movement, the feminist movement, the Black Panthers, CORE (which is an early civil rights movement), the Nicaraguan revolution, and so on. I had come out of the early feminist movement, which involved straight and gay women working together for women's liberation. That movement ended right before ACT UP. It was pretty much destroyed because of internal homophobia and because straight men never really supported it.

In the abortion rights movement, I was involved in direct action, which was a concept that came from Martin Luther King, Gandhi, and the early labor movement. The idea was to actively take an action that creates the condition you need in order to move forward. You are not involved so much in theory, but much more involved in the application of theory to practice. I have lived my whole life creating the action element in which politics come to life. For example, in 1980 Ronald Reagan was elected president, which was the beginning of the horrible period we are still in now. One of the first things he did was to attempt to make abortion illegal. Abortion had only been legal since 1973, so hearings were held in Washington, DC, to try to pass the "Human Life Statute," which would have made abortion and many forms of birth control illegal. During the hearings they would not allow anyone who supported abortion to testify. I was twenty-four at the time and created Women's Liberation Zap Action Brigade with five other women. We went to the hearing, which was on live television, and when a guy testified that a "fetus is an astronaut in a uterine spaceship," we jumped on our chairs with handmade signs, and chanted, "A woman's life is a human life." It was simple but because it was on live television we were seen by millions of people.

CM: And the cameras stayed on you?

SS: Totally. It was my first experience of speaking to people through the media. We received unsolicited donations in the mail from 25,000 people. We had an eleven-day jury trial and were found guilty on the charge of disruption of Congress, but the judge's daughter was a lesbian and the judge gave us probation, so we got away with it. I learned that a very small group of people can have big impact if they get into living rooms and make people part of the conversation.

I got to ACT UP in 1987. I had been covering AIDS since the early 1980s because I was a reporter for the feminist press and gay press in New York. I would go to City Hall and cover the closing of the bathhouses and the very first hearings on AIDS. All of this journalism is collected in one of my books, *My American History*. I published one of the first pieces on women with AIDS in the *Village Voice* as well as the first piece on homeless people with AIDS. As a journalist I was already working on all of this, and I think the Radical Zappers of Feminist and Gay Liberation that had used direct action influenced ACT UP.

CM: Who exactly are the Radical Zappers of Feminist and Gay Liberation?

SS: We did these things called "zaps." For example, homosexuality was considered a psychiatric illness, so Zappers would go to meetings of the American Medical Association, or the American Psychiatric Association, and completely disrupt the meeting by doing something like sitting in the director's office. This was something America had seen during the civil rights movement. A lunch counter would say no Black people could be served and Black people would sit at the counter and perform an action that changes the condition through the action. ACT UP applied this strategic approach consistent with American history. Martin Luther King's piece "Letter from Birmingham Jail" outlines exactly what the ACT UP strategy was. Even though we did not study Dr. King, we absorbed that this was the way to go. First, you highly educate yourself so that you completely understand all the issues, then you propose a solution to the powers that be, a solution that is entirely winnable, reasonable and doable. When they oppose you, they are now in a position where they are unreasonable, so you do direct action to force them, or embarrass them into having to respond to you. That is the strategic sequence and that is how ACT UP was effective.

CM: It seems ACT UP was born out of a radical urgency responding to social and medical conditions surfacing with AIDS. This urgency seems apparent when you equate it to a movement such as the civil rights movement. Has this urgency faded as it concerns gay, lesbian and even trans issues in the United States? What is your perspective of the legacy of ACT UP in the activist field?

SS: Our current problems are not just relative to queer people; they are broad global problems and people in the West are having trouble responding to the political constraints of their governments. As we are speaking right now, there is a revolution in Tunisia; it is very exciting, we do not know what is going to happen, but we are all hoping for the beginning of a wave of democratic movements throughout the Arab world. In the West, however, we have been paralyzed in the last few decades for a lot of reasons. There is very little discussion in the public sphere that is honest about what people's lives are really like or what kinds of solutions are possible. Most honest conversations take place in private, not in public, so the public discourse is very false and paralyzing yet everyone is being bombarded with it, constantly making it difficult to decipher, to look at your own real life and see what it is really like as opposed to what you are told it is like.

Thinking about queers, we are constantly being told that things are so much better and we have made so much progress. I really think we have an enormous amount of change, but change is not the same thing as progress. The way gay people are contained, made secondary, and diminished is far more sophisticated now than it was twenty years ago.

Gay people are being told that the only things they need are marriage and military service and that everything else is fine. We are being told we are completely treated fairly in every way and that we are an integrated part of this country. Thirty years ago, to be antigay was a normative thing. Most people did not know anything about gay people; they did not know they knew gay people, or what gay people's hopes were. Today everybody in this country knows an openly gay person, sees them on television, in their families, and understands what gay people stand for and or want, so to be antigay today is much more dramatically vicious and cruel than it was in the past when you did not know the names and faces of the people you were affecting.

In that context, in the US we have lost every ballot measure, thirty-one out of thirty-one, in the last few years, meaning a huge number of people in this country are viciously antigay and willing to vote antigay. We also have a president who does not support gay people, so we are in a situation where the opposition has a more negative meaning than it did twenty years ago, yet we are supposed to pretend this means nothing and has no impact on us, the real people, our relatives and neighbors. Why are we being told this condition of profound oppression is actually progress? It is not.

Looking at the fields I work in, there is no lesbian play in the American repertoire, there was not one twenty years ago, and there is not one now, is that progress? Or lesbian fiction? I am currently on a panel judging the best lesbian novel of the year. I have read every lesbian novel that has been published this year. A mainstream publisher published one, but the tiniest publishers, so small you can only buy the books online, publish the best. Is that progress? No. I see us being further and further marginalized. Anything that is authentic about what our lives are really like is being more repressed now than it was twenty years ago.

CM: But there has been, however, work coming from gay and lesbian organizations throughout these twenty years. How would you explain complacency within the queer movement in relation to work done by ACT UP, which is to my knowledge the last queer social movement in the US?

SS: ACT UP is the last social movement in the US that effected change regardless of constituency. Maybe to address this question we can think about why ACT UP fell apart, which is complicated. The rate of death was so profound; the dying of leadership and the psychological consequences on members surrounded by mass death for so many years had enormous impact on people.

The election of Clinton was hugely disruptive to building independent activist movements because people gave him too much power and had too much faith in him, so members began working in the Democratic Party and got lost as they became part of the system. There is also the psychological element of wanting to be accepted that is a human impulse I do not want to criticize. As a gay person, you grow up with a lot of rejection. If you think something is happening where the person in charge is going to accept you, give you a better job, have more of a social role, more respect, and earn more money, you go for it. This fulfilled a personal need but the collective movement suffered as a result.

Also the invention of protease inhibitors and AIDS medications, which became available to people who could afford them and lived in a manner in which they were able to manage taking them, those people abandoned all the other people for whom that was not the case. With these substantial structural changes taking place, the consequence was the diminishing of the activist voice and the bureaucracy screwing up in their place. Activists win policy and bureaucrats enact those policies. So, activists won benefits for women with AIDS, which was a four-year campaign by ACT UP, but bureaucrats hand out these benefits, right? Once the activist voice is removed and all you have is the bureaucracy, you cannot make any steps forward, it is impossible. This is the situation we are in now.

In terms of current national groups in the gay movement, they are so conservative because they came out of the Democratic Party. The people who run the Human Rights Campaign (HRC) and all these horrific nightmarish groups that accomplish nothing while spending all this money, these are not the same people who were in ACT UP, they are more identified with the ruling class and structures of power and they like being aligned with all those people. Look at a group like the Gay & Lesbian Alliance Against Defamation (GLAAD); the representation of queer people in arts and entertainment in the United States is hideous. It kills me to watch people going crazy over *Glee*; it is embarrassing, destructive, and humiliating. GLAAD never comments on any of this. All they do is kiss ass to the industry because they want to be within power. This has always been an important psychological factor among queer people, this desperation for the support of people in power. It is like it replaces the rejecting family, the rejecting father.

CM: I have heard the statement that images can be changed through popular culture, but I do not think it is currently a successful strategy in terms of the role people like Ellen DeGeneres really play in effecting social change for people who really need it.

SS: Images can be changed through popular culture, but where is the radical element in popular culture? I know some lesbians who are big agents in Hollywood or producers of crappy television and they do not do anything with this power. They have no apparatus for power, are shortsighted, and only see their own immediate monetary gain. The lust for money is endless. It is not like they get enough and then can do something interesting, they want it forever. There are enough of these people in place already for there to be change but they do not act in unison.

CM: Maybe this is a simplistic comparison, but do you think it has something to do with the fact that during the AIDS crisis there was a literal issue of life and death whereas now people see a social problem they think does not affect people in such a radical way, in the sense that people are not dying?

SS: It is a different kind of death than biological death, absolutely. ACT UP had the entire spectrum of social positions, including people who were disenfranchised and came from no power as well as men who had very elite power and access who were enraged to learn society didn't care about them when they found out they had AIDS. This shock was a lot of their motive, I mean ACT UP is one of these very rare examples in history where privilege and principle coexisted; there was an enormous amount of access and I have never seen a social movement with as much access as ACT UP had even though there were many people in ACT UP who had nothing, who had come out of prison into ACT UP, so it was an incredibly broad coalition.

CM: Was it democratic in its outreach and participation?

SS: It was democratic in its structure in a profound way. If I wanted to do something you did not want to do, you did not try to stop me; you just did what you wanted to do, so there was simultaneity of action as opposed to the old left style, which was that everyone had to agree. With a critical mass of people all being effective in different realms at the same time, you create counterculture. This is the basis for social change from the margins and it is how ACT UP succeeded. But I am also saying many things could be different pretty easily if a very small group of people with access decided to participate differently.

CM: How?

SS: If we go back to popular culture, we can look at the kinds of popular culture being produced. Have you seen this big lesbian movie that is winning all these awards now, *The Kids Are All Right*?

CM: Yes, I saw it this weekend.

SS: It contains a message that lesbian relationships are miserable and emotionally and sexually dead. The movie only shows hot sex with men, the *butch* is mean and makes all the money and the *femme* is a child who cannot finish anything. This is the story of this great new lesbian movie that so many gay people were involved in getting made. It took them many years to get it done, so they all feel great about what they have accomplished, which not only says that these are the only popular messages allowed about lesbian sexuality, but also exposes the amount of involvement and work needed just to get these messages produced. Is this progress? What is different between it and early movies from the 1960s like *The Fox* and *The Killing of Sister George*? There is not much difference across time.

CM: This seems to reflect how popular culture can reinforce heteronormative images. What is your perception of the cultural sector on a smaller scale, the work being done by artists in theater, literature, and visual arts?

SS: Each of those realms is different. Theatre is so conservative in this country it is shocking, and I am an insider. It is an elite art form, has a very tiny audience and no desire to expand that audience. Theatre is obsessed with telling the one story they think is at the center of the culture, which is the coming of age of the white male. That is the story told repeatedly and it is the only story that is seen as important.

Literature is different because it is a mass art form and publishers want to sell as many books as possible to reach a wide audience, so all different kinds of people can publish books, including people of all races and international authors. Still, the dominant apparatus containing this genre remains the white straight male as the emblematic voice of the culture. There are a few exceptions, but they are always decontextualized, like Toni Morrison or someone like that. We went from Hemingway and Fitzgerald to Bellow and Roth, and now we are on to Franzen, so it is always the replaceable straight white male author dominating the culture of publishing,

Cinema is about niche, so there is the Black Queer Film Festival, the Arab American Film Festival, and so on. People cannot get seen in the mainstream, so they produce work at a very low budget. I have been involved now in two lesbian features that were made for $20,000 each. The work is only shown in queer environments and you can't get the money to move the work forward, so it remains a satellite around this impenetrable dominant culture that never sees any of this as part of the world, people who spend their whole lives looking in the mirror and thinking it is a window with no idea what is going on outside.

In terms of gallery and studio art, as far as I can see it at this moment, it has no relationship to most people's lives. I do not think people are going to museums; even when you have a super show like Marina Abramović at the MoMA, my students do not even know, they are not connected in any way. Museums are desperate to try to get younger people to come in. Brooklyn Museum did this show of rock photography trying to get people to come in, but there is a lack of habit and experience of looking at art and expecting to find something that can enrich you. People are so alienated from languages of artists that they do not understand.

CM: I guess it also has to do with reaching an audience. It seems to me that in the last two or three years, New York has had a reemergence of a gender-bending scene. There is a lot of interesting performance work being done, but it is still work that is produced and consumed and appreciated by the downtown scene and subculture. What is your relationship to these subcultures and how do you think they could mobilize?

SS: I have always approached things by creating my own institutions. When Jim Hubbard and I founded the MIX Festival twenty-five years ago, it was because mainstream gay festivals were not showing formally inventive work and the experimental community was not interested in queer work. Now there are people showing in that festival who were not alive when we started it. What we learned is how creating venue creates artists. When people see they can go somewhere and see work that is about them, they become motivated to make work, but if their story is not ever represented, they become alienated from the entire process, so we have done this alternative institution building. Some of the people from MIX have gone on to great things.

Two of the curators who we supported are now running MoMA and Sundance and bringing a queer eye to these spaces and larger institutions. For some people it has been a stepping stone but I also went to MIX this year and it was packed with hundreds of young artists who were there to show and see work rather than network, make professional connections, money, and deals. This is incredible, as someone who created the institution, to see hundreds of young people participating in seeing and making experimental work.

CM: Is this similar to what you were saying in terms of a larger scope of popular culture? For these institutions and propositions to be created by people with access?

SS: Sure, of course.

CM: So what is stopping this type of progress? Is there still a backdrop or notion of morality permeating everything?

SS: No, there is an incredible fear and I see it in every field. This is a time of incredible conformity and everyone, including teachers and writers, whatever their role, [is] terrified about making power structures over them uncomfortable. They fear losing access, money, and respect. Everything is run by fear so people are afraid of alienating the powers that be and trying interesting new things, because they are afraid someone is going to look down on them and they will no longer be invited to the party. In the trans scene they are creating their own party, which is really the only way to do it because it is very hard to change institutions. That is why we build alternative institutions.

CM: You talk about the notion of fear in relation to homophobia in your book *Ties That Bind*. It seems fear is so intertwined and conditioned by family structures and the impact of religion upon the fabrics of this society. Can you speak about where this fear comes from?

SS: Sure, familial homophobia is reflected by larger societal structures. In a family, one child is being victimized by the parents for being gay, whereas the other children have a choice. The heterosexual children can risk being alienated from their parents by standing up for their sibling or they can be complicit with the victimization and earn the approval of their parents; that is how familial homophobia works. This is the emblematic model of the whole culture. For example, where I teach, when we hired one Black person, some of the white people were okay with that, but when we wanted to hire three, it was too many. When you start pushing the envelope and trying to diversify faculty by identifying qualified people who bring what is needed to the department, white people panic. They are afraid they are going to lose their access and privileges. That is the same structure as familial homophobia. You have people with enormous amounts of money, so much money they will never be poor no matter what they do, but they are afraid of doing anything independent with any teeth because they do not want the disapproval of the people in power.

I am afraid too. I am frightened all the time, but I do not let the fears determine my behavior. How I act and whether or not I am afraid are two separate things in my process. I think questions such as, is this doable, reasonable, and morally sound? What are the consequences going to be when I do this? I know I will make some people mad but can I actually achieve something positive? If I think I can be effective, I allow myself to feel afraid. The problem is when people act because they are afraid. These two things need to be separated. It is okay to feel uncomfortable. If you are going to create anything worthy, you are going to feel uncomfortable and other people are going to make you feel uncomfortable, and that has to be accepted as part of life. If you want to feel safe all the time, you will never be able to do anything.

CM: Do you think the existence of fear within the family has to do with the primacy of the nuclear family as a structure and its relationship to religious ethics or morality?

SS: I do not think it is so theoretical, I think it is just really your reality.

CM: How can we change it?

SS: In my book I argue for a third-party intervention. Right now we privilege the family. If your gay friend tells you his family has done this terrible thing to him, you say: "Oh I am so sorry, let's go out for a drink." You should instead call the family and say: "I love your son, I have been his friend for thirty years and you do not know anything about his life, and I am here with twenty other people who would like to come to your house and explain to you why it is not acceptable to us that you treat him this way."

CM: That is confronting fear from both ends, right?

SS: Yes, but it is mainly telling them we no longer privilege the family as the ultimate authority. For example, the Catholic Church had gotten on the public-school boards in New York City to pass rules against distributing condoms in public schools, though their children primarily attended Catholic schools. ACT UP realized people would die because of what the Catholic Church was doing and that we had a moral right to go into their church and interrupt their mass. We went to St. Patrick's Cathedral and stopped the church in one of ACT UP's famous direct actions. Today, you can get condoms in public schools and people's lives have been saved because we took that action. At this time people asked how we could go into a church to disrupt mass, and we believed gay people's lives equaled the church, that the church was not more important than gay people's lives, and that is the attitude we need to take with families and not just with the families of our friends. As a teacher, I tell my students in Staten Island who live with terrible homophobia to bring in their parents for me to meet with. I can wear my suit, be the professor, they come sit in my office, and I can explain to them why they are wrong. The voice of authority has to intervene.

That is what arts and entertainment could be doing, but they are not. What they tell us is that everyone loves and tolerates gay people, the gay person is the best friend of the important straight person who gets to have a romance and that gay people are only nervous or upset because they have internalized fear. That is what movies are telling us all the time.

CM: Maybe except for Anderson Cooper who does not seem to be publicly out, but he does confront homophobes quite strongly in his program.

SS: I do not watch him. But what does it mean if you are in the closet and you do that? It is strange.

CM: It is strange but he is still sending a message, I would say.

SS: But the message is to stay in the closet, or that only closeted, straight people can get on television. Look at Susan Sontag; she wrote the book *AIDS and Its Metaphors* while she was in the closet. How can you write anything meaningful about AIDS if you are in the closet? What is gained by staying in the closet? Money and fame?

CM: It is very discouraging.

SS: I am optimistic because I have learned to set my own agenda and create my own institutions. We started the ACT UP Oral History Project to create a space for telling this history. No one will be able to say they cannot find this history anymore, and we are making a feature film and moving the material forward, and we are just two people. Two people can do a great deal. Also, working to bring leaders of the queer Palestinian movement to the US, I did this on my own with just my phone.

CM: Can you speak more about this new project?

SS: I was invited to give a lecture in Israel during the Lesbian and Gay Studies Conference at Tel Aviv University. I was made aware of an academic boycott in which people were being asked not to go to state-sponsored institutions in Israel. I talked to a number of Jewish academics in Israel who asked me not to speak at the conference but to decline and support the boycott, coming instead for a solidarity visit. I declined and instead went to Tel Aviv and spoke at an anarchist vegan café. Sixty people attended and we had a good conversation that included many people who would have been at the conference.

CM: What did you talk about?

SS: I talked about why I declined and I talked about homophobia in the family, which everyone can relate to. Then I spoke at the Haifa Women's Center and with a Palestinian lesbian organization and an Israeli Jewish women's peace group. I went to the West Bank, met an LGBT group and spoke to the people organizing the boycott. I told them my concerns about them not being supportive enough of gay people. From this meeting the queers I met and I decided I would organize a trip for them to come to America and speak to the LGBT community here because people don't know there is a Palestinian queer movement, or don't understand there is a secular, pro-gay, feminist sector of Palestinians who are supporting economic sanctions as a nonviolent strategy for change. We should be supporting these people, so I wanted to introduce them to the gay community here. Since last April, it is now February; I have organized six cities to host them with different public events.

CM: It is a form of direct action in a way.

SS: Totally, completely.

CM: Can you speak more about the ACT UP Oral History Project, as you seem to be constructing a story that has been neglected or has not been written? Can you speak about this project, the intention behind it, and the process making it?

SS: In 2001, it was the twentieth anniversary of AIDS, so we are in the thirtieth year of AIDS today. I was in Los Angeles driving around in my rental car listening to NPR, and the woman said America initially had trouble with people with AIDS but eventually came around. I felt this was inaccurate, thinking about all these people who were dead and had fought to their last breath to force this country to change against its will. The dead were being falsely historicized as though this country was so benevolent, that it had naturally evolved, false progress yet again, and I thought, I could not let this happen.

I called Jim because we had collaborated in ACT UP, we had created MIX, and we decided to start interviewing surviving members of ACT UP and make a record. We got a lot of financial support from people who had been activists with us twenty years before who now worked in philanthropy, and we both had enormous personal credibility from our earlier experiences with people who knew we were hard-working and would follow through, so we were given money by the ACT UP community. I have interviewed people with whom I was a political enemy in ACT UP, but the interviews go very well because we are working together for the common goal to have honest history of how this country came to change. Part of the message is also that regular people can make change, that regular people who worked in furniture stores and were bookkeepers drove ACT UP.

Now, over ten years, we have done 128 long-form interviews. I conduct almost all the interviews and Jim and our friend James Wentzy do the camera work, like a little mom-and-pop business. We put transcripts up on the website to download because our whole thing is about providing this information free. We have always wanted to make things available and accessible. Eighty thousand people have downloaded transcripts, so we tried to find out where they were from and a lot of them are from Eastern Europe and Asia, so we think we are reaching people with AIDS in countries that have no AIDS activist movement and are trying to get information.

In the process of doing this, Jim collected 2,000 hours of archival footage; the camcorder was invented in the middle of the ACT UP movement, so you have Super 8 film cameras and 16 mm film cameras, some of which are black-and-white. There was no way to record off a television set, so they aimed the camera at the television to capture TV footage. Then you move to early video, Beta, High 8, all these different formats. We took all of it and digitized it so when you look at it, it looks like a dream. It is incredible and of course it made video activism possible, which is a good lesson to activists about using new technologies, but not being consumed by them. I used Facebook and Skype to do this Palestinian thing, but I do not feel like it controlled me; I feel like I was able to use it to reach my political goals. Now we are doing a feature film called *United in Anger: A History of ACT UP*, where we are combining the interview footage with the archival footage so you see somebody today talking about an action they did and see the footage of them doing it. It is wonderful, very exciting.

CM: When you conduct interviews with people, what angle do you take? Is it personal stories or is it the way they remember their involvement in the organization?

SS: They take different levels of responsibility to prepare for the interviews; some people really take it seriously and review all their materials and decide what they want to make record. Others are very cavalier, have not thought about it for five minutes, just sit down, and can't remember anything, but that is who they are, this is their one opportunity to make record and some people just cannot do it. Still, I try to get as much out of them as I can. We ask about who they were before they came to ACT UP, and that has been really fascinating because people have almost nothing in common and come from entirely different value systems, different ranges of experiences with politics or no experience with AIDS. There are straight people who did not know a single person with AIDS who joined ACT UP and became amazing activists, so it took us a really long time to figure out what these people may have in common. After eight years we figured out this is a certain type of person who cannot sit there and watch a gross injustice take place in front of them without doing something about it. For this reason, all these diverse people at one moment in their lives did the right thing, and that is what they have in common. It seems many of them have never done anything of value since ACT UP, for some people it began a lifelong service, and others they were already on that track and it was just another thing they did to be a responsible citizen, so it is very diverse in that regard.

Interview with Writer Sarah Schulman

Marissa Bell Toffoli / 2011

From wordswithwriters.com, December 27, 2011. Reprinted with permission of the author.

Sarah Schulman's books include the novels *Rat Bohemia*, *Empathy*, and *The Child*, and the nonfiction book *Ties That Bind: Familial Homophobia and Its Consequences*. She is codirector of the ACT UP Oral History Project, and she is currently organizing the first US LGBT delegation to Palestine for Winter 2012. Sarah is a Distinguished Professor of the Humanities at CUNY, College of Staten Island, and was awarded a Brown Foundation Fellowship from the Museum of Fine Arts, Houston. Her other awards include a Guggenheim, a Fulbright, and the 2009 Kessler Award for her "Sustained Contribution to LGBT Studies."

Quick Facts

- Home: Manhattan, New York
- Comfort food: Well, I'm in San Francisco. I like the burritos with salsa verde at Alabama and 24th Street. That would be my San Francisco comfort food.
- Top reads: Carson McCullers, Rabih Alameddine, Caryl Phillips, Vivian Gornick, and Claudia Rankine. I like *Funeral Rites* by Jean Genet.
- Current reads: *Lady Painter*, the Joan Mitchell biography by Patricia Albers; *Open City* by Teju Cole

Marissa Bell Toffoli: What are you working on at the moment?

Sarah Schulman: Well, I'm working on a lot of things. I have a book coming out in the fall of 2012 from Duke University Press called *Israel/Palestine* *and the Queer International*. It's a political memoir that's basically about how the rise of the gay movement in Palestine is going to transform secular politics in Palestine, and that's going to transform Arab politics and therefore global politics. I am predicting and feeling that it's a key movement to emerge at a very key time. I'm anticipating a lot of great consequences as a result.

I just finished a new novel. It's called *The Cosmopolitans*. I wanted it to sound like a Henry James novel. It's a remake of Balzac's *Cousin Bette*. *Cousin Bette* is about a spinster who is wronged by her family and wants to get revenge. She destroys everybody and everything, and in the end, she wins. That was the plot I started with, but I set it in Greenwich Village in 1958. I was born that year, and it's set in the building I was born in, and in fact it ends on the day of my birth.

In the process of writing, it also became an answer book to a second novel, which is James Baldwin's *Another Country*. Because of the milieu and the time, *The Cosmopolitans* is about interraciality, bohemianism; it's about straight people and gay people interacting with each other. Suddenly I ended up in the same territory as Baldwin's *Another Country*, only the difference was that my female characters are real and his aren't. I thought, wow, this is a book that's speaking to both Balzac and Baldwin at the same time. I'm really happy with it. I've been working on it since 2003.

MBT: Where did the idea for *The Mere Future* come from?

SS: I had this sentence: "Passion escapes me on the hot sun porch." I just had that and I didn't know what to do with it. I believe it became the words of the article that the main character writes about Glick. She's only allowed eight words for the article. That's what I started with, and I just started justifying it. I was feeling very free.

I've written seventeen books and each book is in a different style. But I've written another book that has a similar impulse to this one, which is called *Empathy* and came out in 1992. It was also highly formally inventive. I think form really has to come organically from the emotions at the core of the piece. Sometimes you're just in a territory where nothing that's known is appropriate for that content, or that emotional impulse, so you have to invent it.

In this case, since the subject is the future, you can't really write a novel about the future using language of the past. It doesn't make any sense. I guess Anthony Burgess proved that in *A Clockwork Orange*. But what is the language of our future? And it's the mere future, not the far future. I wanted it to be like something that we're on the precipice of linguistically. There's texting fragments and email, and all that. Then, there's the incredible speed with which slogans and marketing and advertising creep into conversation, and people internalize that. And then, there's like channel surfing, where you can completely understand what's happening in two or three words. So many of the paradigms in entertainment are repetitive and you can trigger them with very few words; they don't have to be full sentences. All of that is the language of the future. It's a language of reduction. But I didn't want to just do that, because it's boring—it's flat. I took that kind of minimal, associative, reductive language, but I made it sort of funny and interesting, and a little smarter than it normally would be. I stylized it up. That's how the language part came to be.

You know, it was written in 1999. It took ten years to find a publisher. It looks like it's about Obama, but it actually had nothing to do with that. I was writing about the future, and there were certain trends that I could see were coming, and people who were reading the manuscript couldn't see that those trends were coming. It was only when the trends had actually already come that those people could then understand the book. It sort of defeated the purpose of it, but I've had that experience before. Sometimes I write with a ten-year gap.

MBT: What do you hope readers will take away from *The Mere Future*?

SS: Of course, I want them to enjoy it. I would like them to feel okay about reading slowly. It's not a long book, but some of the sentences require thought. You can't glide over it; it's not a skimming kind of book. You know, I once read Colette's autobiography and it took me three years. And I think that's okay. It's like the slow food movement, but it's the slow read movement.

MBT: Who do you picture as the ideal reader of your work?

SS: I think there are all different kinds of readers, but two in particular that I notice. One really wants to be told things that they already know. They find that very comforting. They want familiarity, which they've confused with quality. If it's not already known, they become angry and frustrated, and they think it's bad or wrong or they reject it.

Then there are readers who, if you offer them something they've never seen before, they're ecstatic; they live for that. And that is my ideal reader, just in general. They want the experience of being expanded. I kind of think that's the difference between art and entertainment. People come home from work and they turn on the TV to not expand, to live in a state of repetition, familiarity, and comfort. But art is something that changes you, it doesn't just repeat.

MBT: Where and when do you prefer to write?

SS: I can really write anywhere. Given the quantity of how much I write, I'd better be able to. I don't have a set time or anything like that. It's always been that way.

MBT: Where would you most want to live and write?

SS: Well, I love New York City. I was born there and I'm a second-generation New Yorker. My expectation is that I'll die there. I really don't want to live anywhere else. I live in a six-floor walk-up, and one of my dreams is to live in an apartment with an elevator.

MBT: What do you listen to when you work?

SS: It depends on what phase of writing I'm doing. I rewrite a lot; I'll do like ten to twelve drafts of something. For rewriting, definitely NPR. For composing, either NPR or nothing. It's like white noise.

MBT: Do you have a philosophy for how and why you write?

SS: How I write? I think I'm a natural. I experience it entirely as biology, some kind of a neuron thing. I don't attribute it to any kind of will or character discipline, or anything like that.

Why? I don't know. It's my natural state. It's like I'm an animal and that's just how I do things. I've written so much, and I started writing when I was six. I spent my whole life writing, and that's how I live. It's not like I don't do anything else, but it's easy for me. I just do it a lot and, I don't know, it's a way of life. It's like people who know how to sing—they just sing. I don't have that. I'll never have it.

MBT: How do you balance content with form?

SS: It's always been an organic relationship, even before I knew that was the case. With my first book, I remember I was interviewed in 1984, and someone said, "I see you used pastiche," and I said, "What is pastiche?" Somehow I had a postmodern impulse, but I always thought it was because I was uneven. I kept trying to make it even, and I couldn't. Then I found out that was postmodern and that it was okay.

The more I've learned about form, the more I understand the choices I have. There have been times when I've said, all right, I'm going to try to write a bestseller. I go to the store, and I try to pick out the least obnoxious bestseller, and then I can't read it. I'll think, I'll just write something that's even, but I've never been able to.

MBT: Is there a quote about writing that inspires you?

SS: Audre Lorde was my college professor. She told my class to write this down: "That you can't fight City Hall is a rumor being spread by City Hall." That's one of my mottos. You might think it's not about writing, but it is. The only reason you think you have to do things a certain way is because the people who are invested in it being that way are telling you that. It doesn't mean it's true.

MBT: What advice would you give to aspiring writers?

SS: Well, it really depends on the person. It's so hard. Do you mean professionally or artistically? I mean, I hate MFA programs; I think they're terrible for the culture and that they hurt people's writing. On the other hand, if you are a working-class person or an unconnected person, you have to get an MFA. Even if you do, there's no guarantee. I teach in a City University of New York, and my students are mostly working class, and I've sent like three students to MFA programs in twelve years. Very few have gone. Those students have been ultragifted, but then when they get there, they're so fish-out-of-water because they're the wrong class, and the teachers don't mentor them. So even though they get the MFA, they still can't get the goodies from it. But if they don't get that, forget it. I think in class terms, you have to have it. If you come from the upper middle class, or upper classes, if you have connections and relationships in the social apparatus, perhaps you don't need it.

In terms of artistically, the best way to be an artist is to make art, see art, and talk about art with other artists. If you're a writer, I'd say read, go to readings, write a lot, meet other people and talk to them about what they're doing. That way, you accrue eclectic influences, and that's the most important thing. The problem with an MFA program is that it homogenizes people's influences. If you accrue eclectic influences, you have a much better chance of crafting something that's organic to you. The groupthink is antithetical to what our practice is as writers; that's the problem—homogenization and the branding.

I was very lucky that I met many wonderful, fantastic writers and talked to them, and have had conversations with them all my life. I pulled it together that way, and that's been very special.

MBT: What's the best advice you've been given as a writer?

SS: I was a waitress for ten years, and I had published two books. Not only did I not go get an MFA, I had never even heard of an MFA. It's an age thing. The MFA just wasn't the thing at that time. I was a waitress in the first coffee shop in Tribeca. So Tribeca was gentrifying, and certain artists were coming in for breakfast because it was the only coffee shop. I waited on Yvonne Rainer, and Meredith Monk, and Isabella Rossellini, and all these people, for their eggs. A lot of these artists would talk to me, and I told them that I'd published two novels, and they told me that I needed to get an MFA.

I enrolled in this city college program, which actually was an MA, but I didn't know the difference. I go the first day, and the teacher was Grace Paley. She has everybody go around the room and read something that they're writing. I was writing my third novel, and it was a first-person lesbian narrator. The other students thought that the narrator was a man, and I thought, oh no, this is going to be two years of hell. I got really scared. After class, Grace was like, "Sarah, come to my office." So I go to her office and she goes, "Look, you're really a writer. You're really doing it. You don't need this class. Go home." I went home; I never went back. Well, she completely saved me, because I would have been destroyed by that. It was the best thing anyone ever, ever said to me. I'm so grateful, my whole life, for that.

MBT: What do you find most challenging about writing?

SS: I have too many ideas. I'm behind, like, years behind. I want to hurry up. Now I'm fifty-three, I can see the clock is ticking. I've ramped it up a lot. This year, I had two new paperbacks, and two new hardcovers come out. But I really have a lot of things I want to do.

MBT: When you're not writing, what do you like to do?

SS: I like to consume art. I live in a world where I have a lot of friends who are artists. So, I like to see work that my friends have made or that they're in, or talk to them about what they're making, or read what they're doing, go to their studios and rehearsals. I do a lot of that, and look at cuts of their movies and talk to them about it. I just love being involved in all of that.

One of my favorite things about New York City is that it's one of the places where ideas originate. You hear the idea and you engage in it with the person who is originating it. It may be years before that idea is a product that somebody else can buy on a bookshelf or see in a movie theater.

And I'm a teacher, so I have a full-time job. I'm very invested in some of my kids. I care a lot about what happens to them, and a lot of my kids are in a lot of trouble, and they have all kinds of problems, so I have to really care. This is at a city university.

An Interview with Sarah Schulman

Zoe Whittall / 2013

From *The Believer*, February 2013. Reprinted with permission of the author.

In the spring of 2012, Sarah Schulman invited me to her partner's Toronto home on a rainy Saturday afternoon. The partnership being somewhat new and long-distance, she moved about the space a bit awkwardly, claiming she had never spent much time in a house before, having lived in Manhattan for fifty-three years, and in the same sixth-floor walk-up in the East Village for the past thirty. "In New York City, if you want privacy, you just sit in the same room and don't talk. This house thing is very new to me." She made me a cup of tea and we sat in the living room with my iPhone recorder between us on the ottoman.

At the time, her fifth nonfiction book, *Israel/Palestine and the Queer International*, was the forthcoming lead title from Duke University Press, and she was in Toronto for the launch of *The Gentrification of the Mind: Witness to a Lost Imagination*. Her documentary, *United in Anger: A History of ACT UP*, had just premiered in New York City. But while Schulman is many things—an accomplished political activist, a distinguished professor, filmmaker, playwright, and general cultural agitator—her primary love is writing fiction. When we met, she had just finished writing her tenth literary novel, *The Cosmopolitans*, which she described to me as "an answer book to Baldwin's *Another Country* and a response to Balzac's *Cousin Bette*," set in New York City in 1958.

A gifted storyteller, Schulman has spent much of her career chronicling queer lives. She approaches fiction with a fearlessness regarding both form and content, and possesses an unflinching ability to create nuanced, emotional characters while simultaneously crafting stories that embody the political and cultural complexity of America at its most unrepresented. Her versatility as a writer is proven with each new story she puts out, whether she's embracing her own imaginative take on literary realism or jumping into satirical speculative fiction, as she did with her latest novel, *The Mere Future*. She is best known for her widely praised, groundbreaking 1995 novel, *Rat Bohemia*, which was set in the swirl of the AIDS crisis in New York City.

While many writers of her generation are content to stay coyly closeted—too many prominent best-selling American writers to mention—Schulman has steadfastly refused. As a result, her status as a cultural pioneer and icon to aspiring queer writers has been cemented, while her literary career has, on occasion, suffered. As the publishing industry has grown more conservative, her last two novels were difficult to place. When recounting the plot of her latest literary manuscript, *The Cosmopolitans*, she acknowledges: "It's an opportunity for me to return to mainstream publishing, if they'll have me."

I. Loving Mentor

The Believer: I want to talk about your experiences trying to publish your novel *The Child*. It seems to me as though America is in a period of deep sexual regression right now. I mean, the right to acquire birth control is actually up for debate. What was the process like, trying to publish it in this climate?

Sarah Schulman: It was a nightmare. First of all, I had been publishing a book almost every two years since forever, and suddenly I was stopped dead. People would stop me on the street and ask, "What's happening with you? I haven't seen any books by you." And I would say, "It exists! They just won't let you have it." I was sending it around as samizdat. I would print it out and give it to people. This was in 1999, before Kindles. It was awful. So many bad things happened. An editor at Beacon read it and really loved the book and told me she was going to buy it. She made an offer, but her editor in chief vetoed it because she said it was supporting child abuse. Finally, one day I ran into Diamanda Galás in the neighborhood. She asked me why I hadn't published in so long. I explained that I had written a novel about a sexual relationship between a fifteen-year-old boy and a forty-year-old man, from their points of view, and that since I didn't condemn the relationship, it was unpublishable. She took out her cell phone and called Don Weise at Carroll & Graf on the spot. "This is Diamanda Galás," she said. "I'm sending you Sarah Schulman's new novel. Treat this sister with respect." Don ended up publishing the book, but, typically for the book business, Carroll & Graf went out of business the week *The Child* was published. They printed it, but it wasn't reviewed or distributed. Fortunately, Arsenal Pulp Press in Canada published the paperback, but the book never got its moment, which is very sad for me since I love it. I think it would make a great movie.

Believer: Was it hard to inhabit any of the characters creatively, or to have empathy for them? Do you believe writers have to have empathy for their characters?

Schulman: It wasn't hard to have empathy for the characters. My job is to figure out what is it like for these people to be alive. What is their perspective on their own experience? That's my job because I'm a novelist. But because I did my job, it made the book unpublishable, because I saw that there were positive aspects to the experience for both of them. The kid's parents were so homophobic and awful that the fact that he had a sexual relationship with an adult man was, in a way, an antidote to his relationship with his father. It wasn't a desirable relationship—the man in the book is very childish and can't take responsibility for things, but the kid got many positive things out of it. What caused him pain was not his boyfriend, but his parents and the state. And that's not what the message is supposed to be. The message is supposed to be the evil, child-abusing predator, blah blah blah. I had the wrong message. I was in a state of perpetual censorship for almost ten years.

Believer: In a recent interview, the *New York Times* said that you were a loving mentor to many young writers. Do you agree with that?

Schulman: Yes, I do agree with that. I'm very supportive of young artists. I treat them with respect, especially queer artists. I want them to do well. Because somebody has to care.

Believer: Did you have mentors when you were young?

Schulman: Grace Paley famously helped me by sending me home after my first and only day of an MFA program. That was truly great. But mentor as in sitting down and reading the books and helping me professionally? There wasn't anyone. It wasn't like there was some lesbian writer who had published mainstream books and had access to stuff who could help me. There wasn't such a person. The generation before me is, like, Susan Sontag... they were just in the closet. My generation is the first to be completely out in popular culture. The people before me couldn't and wouldn't help me. The ones who didn't have access, because they were out, couldn't help me. The ones who did have access, had access because they were in the closet, so they wouldn't. I found out later that behind the scenes people do do things. I got into MacDowell in 1986, and years later I found out that Tillie Olsen was one of the people who supported my application. So that's cool. I never met her, but that was nice. Edmund White did me a huge favor by writing that review in the *New York Times* of *Rat Bohemia*. That was extremely supportive and kind of him. Kathy Acker wrote a really nice review of *After Delores* in the *Village Voice*, and I didn't know her. She did it just because she liked the book.

Believer: Tell me about the group of young writers that you host in your apartment.

Schulman: I did a reading at Bluestockings in New York City about four years ago, and there was a big discussion afterward about how frustrated I was that younger lesbian writers are not having lesbian content in their work. I know why they're not doing it: because you can't have a career if you have it. But unless people keep submitting that material, it's never going to change. What we see is really bad-quality work, because the most talented writers are escaping the content. The literature gets destroyed. I was talking about how MFA programs are a really obstructive force in the development of lesbian fiction, because most of them don't have faculty who actually understand how it works and who can actually give informed support to their students. I mean, you know this. There are all kinds of representational and aesthetic questions in writing lesbian fiction that are very specific. The English language is constructed around a male-female dichotomy, so just having two "she's" in one sentence is something that has to be finessed, right? Then there is the balance of characters. When I wrote *People in Trouble*, I had a straight male protagonist and I had a lesbian protagonist. Balancing them was almost impossible, because anything she did, she would be seen as pathological, but anything he did, the reader could excuse. Having them in the same scene was so hard because he could do anything and she couldn't do anything. All that stuff—you need people who can understand that. MFA programs don't provide that. Lesbian writers who go into them end up producing material that doesn't have any primary lesbian content. Ellis Avery was my graduate student. You can actually trace who the exceptions are, and see who they studied with. So I was talking about that, how upsetting it was, and the audience was quite young. Someone said, "You should start a group!" or, "Put your money where your mouth is!" I said OK. I passed around a sign-up sheet and I called everyone who signed up and invited them over to my house. I live in a very small apartment. About ten girls came over to my apartment. I didn't know any of these people. They crammed into my living room. I didn't do any screening. It's turned out to be a wonderful experience for me.

Believer: What do you get out of the experience?

Schulman: They're very interesting. I love to watch the ways they help each other. They're quite smart. They're very different. Their work is very engaging. They struggle. They rewrite. One of the rules is that once we agree on a date and time, no one is allowed to cancel. You can't come late and you can't cancel—no matter what. I got a free trip to China and I came home early because I had promised the date. If you keep all your promises, you can be very productive. If you say that you're going to come here on this time and this day and bring a work that is four to ten pages—and you do it because you said you would—you will produce work.

II. "So We Got a Camera"

Believer: Can you describe for me how the ACT UP Oral History Project and the documentary *United in Anger: A History of ACT UP* came to be?

Schulman: It was 2001. I was in LA trying to get a job in television or movies. That's already funny. I was in a white rental car, and I can barely drive. It was the twentieth anniversary of AIDS. NPR was talking about it, and somebody said, "At first, America had trouble with people with AIDS, but then they came around." And I just thought, That is not what happened. There's this American tendency to falsely naturalize change that people fight for and earn with their last drop of blood. America pretends that we just naturally evolved. We've always been that way. But in this case, because so many of our friends are dead, and they're not here to speak for themselves, we do have a special responsibility. It's one thing if everyone who participates in a social transformation somehow collectively decides not to contest the historicization, but when the people who did are not here, and they don't have that option, there is a special responsibility. I remember thinking, They're going to do this to AIDS. They're going to pretend that all these thousands of people who fought until their death never suffered, never coalesced, and that it was by the graces of the beautiful dominant culture that suddenly we were all so understanding. I couldn't bear the thought of it. I called Jim Hubbard. We had been collaborators since 1987, and we decided we would start an oral history project. At that point, no one remembered ACT UP, except for the people who'd been part of it. There was no discussion about AIDS; AIDS was over. AIDS activism was barely mentioned. I mean, Benjamin Shepard had written a book called *From ACT UP to the WTO*—I think that was the only modern engagement with ACT UP. So we got a camera and we wrote a grant to try to get software to start interviewing people. Lo and behold, Urvashi Vaid was at the Ford Foundation. Years ago, she had been the head of the National Gay and Lesbian Task Force. At that time, it was considered to be the most conservative gay organization. It was to the left of the Democratic Party. There were no right-wing gay people at that time. Being in the Democratic Party was considered conservative.

Believer: This was pre–Log Cabin Republicans…

Schulman: It was pre-everything. It's pre–Human Rights Campaign, pre–Don't Ask, Don't Tell. We were the street politic people. They were the policy people. We weren't that far apart, but we felt like we were. So she helped us write the grant proposal, and we were able to get three hundred thousand dollars. It was her vision. She knew that we could do this huge thing. To date, we've interviewed 128 people. Long-form interviews. Everything is available for free online at the website actuporalhistory.org. We've sold the archive to Harvard. The agreement is they will make it available for free in perpetuity in all future formats, so let's say everything switches to HD; they're going to have to switch it to HD. This is the kind of thing we could not do. Before that, all the tapes were in Jim's office. He's sixty-three. I'm fifty-three. If we got hit by a bus, that would be it. It was too much responsibility. This turns out to be the perfect solution. That's how it started. We couldn't take it. We couldn't take that thought of it being falsely historicized. Now there is a little moment going on where other people are making it work. That's really what cultural activism is: you take the void and transform it into a context. It's not carpetbagging, where you look for a context and jump on it. It's starting from nothing. We did the same thing with the MIX festival. There was no venue for gay, experimental film in 1987, so we invented one. Twenty-five years later, we have people showing work in our festival who were not born when we started it. What we learned is that creating a venue creates artists, because people see the venue and think, Oh, I can make something for that. Then they become artists. That's really what cultural activism is. It's not exploiting other people's work. It's doing the labor from the ground up.

III. The Ghost World and the World

Believer: I want to talk about the idea of deaths that matter and deaths that don't, which you write about so eloquently in *The Gentrification of the Mind.* You said, "The deaths of these 81,542 New Yorkers, who were despised and abandoned, who did not have rights or representation, who died because of the neglect of their government and families, has been ignored. This gaping hole of silence has been filled by the deaths of 2,752 people murdered by outside forces. The disallowed grief of twenty years of AIDS deaths was replaced by ritualized and institutionalized mourning of the acceptable dead. In this way, 9/11 is the gentrification of AIDS. The replacement of deaths that don't matter with deaths that do." How did you come to this conclusion? Have you taken any heat for it, or any of the other things you say in the book?

Schulman: No heat, except *Publishers Weekly* said I was vitriolically against motherhood. Women who question parenting are always the witch. [*Laughs*] I live on 9th Street. I saw the World Trade Center thing happen from my roof. When the building went down, I got on my bike and I went to St. Vincent's Hospital to give blood. On my way there, I was watching these people in business suits walking up from Wall Street covered in ash. When I got to St. Vincent's, there was a line around the block. So many people had had the same thought and just ran there. But there was no need to give blood, because everyone was dead. It was a weird, ghostly thing. Then they closed off the city at 14th Street. We had free access, if you lived downtown. I biked to the World Trade Center. You could watch. Everything was burning. Everyone was so shocked. It was so strange. The first thing I thought was—this was when we were bombing Bosnia—I remember thinking that Americans were finally going to understand what it's like; what we do to other people. That was my first thought. This will be an incredible wake-up. The next day, people came looking for the corpses. And because most of the people who died were either cops or firefighters or traders, the people who came to Manhattan to look for their dead people were from Queens and Staten Island and New Jersey. They were bringing these American flags, they were putting up signs: have you seen my person? And it just suddenly turned. It could have been this moment of compassion, understanding, and revelation, and it became this patriotic nightmare. Bush went on TV and said, "They are evil and we are good." Everyone was stunned and in shock. I thought, This is so how I felt during AIDS, emotionally, and now everyone is feeling it. That thought stayed with me the whole time. Later, I found out that only two people I knew had died. One was the mother of a friend from ACT UP, and one was the husband of an actress I knew. So in all of those thousands of people who died, it didn't reach my people. It was like AIDS in reverse. Back then, I knew all these people who were sick and dying, and then I'd meet some straight person and they didn't know anybody. I started to think about these two things as like, the ghost world and the world: two sides of the same situation, but infecting entirely different populations. As the whole schtick around 9/11 evolved, and the war in Iraq, I always kept that in mind. AIDS was one version and 9/11 was the other.

IV. The Apparatus

Believer: I read *The Gentrification of the Mind* within months of reading *Just Kids* by Patti Smith and *Inferno* by Eileen Myles. They feel like excellent companion pieces to yours. My experience of New York City is limited—I have spent only a total of seventy-two hours there, as a tourist. But reading these books and yours in succession felt like I was taking a course in what it was like to be an artist in the New York City of the 1970s to the 1990s. What did you think of those books?

Schulman: I loved *Inferno*. I think it's her best book. I love her work. It's funny, sexy, it's got a history of the New York School, it draws its own literary genealogy. I hated *Just Kids*. I felt it was very disingenuous. She made herself very clean. She's a good person because she was understanding that her boyfriend was gay. Yet he ended up being pimped by a rich guy, whom she kind of pimped off also. She doesn't like women at all. Every man she dates ends up being incredibly connected and powerful, and propels her professionally. She has a high ick factor around lesbians. The only woman she mentions is Sandy Daley, an experimental filmmaker who made the film *Robert Having His Nipple Pierced*, which we showed at MIX. She seems to have instinctively stayed away from women who don't have any power, and gone with men who had enormous amounts of power. I was shocked to discover that, because Patti Smith was my hero!

Believer: Feminists love Patti!

Schulman: She wrote all that great lesbian stuff in her songs, apparently none of which is real. I quote it in *After Delores*. None of it was true. I was crushed when I read that book. But I loved Eileen's book.

Believer: Your style is not stagnant, and it changes often, but it was quite a switch to speculative fiction with your dystopian novel, *The Mere Future*. The villain, Harrison Bond, is a parody of a depressed celebrity author, and he's writing a book called *My Sperm*. Was he based on anyone?

Schulman: When I was writing this, I was at Yaddo. When I arrived, there were five male writers there: Tom Beller, Donald Antrim, Rick Moody, Jeffrey Eugenides—and was it Jonathan Franzen? No, I can't remember. It was of that ilk. I arrived with my suitcase and they were sitting on the porch and smoking cigars. I said, "I can't believe you guys are smoking cigars." And the guys said, "Paul Auster showed us how." I spent the summer with them. At that point, I had published maybe eight books, and they each had one or two. And they had no interest in me. They had no respect for me. The worst of the lot became Harrison Bond. He's a type. Gish Jen was there, too. She's an Asian American writer who at one point had a lot of currency and success. At that time, she was really up there. We were at dinner, and it was me and this gay Filipino guy, and we asked her, "What's it like to be up there with all the guys?" That was the era of the Rick Moodys of the world. She said, pointing to us three, "We are the center of the culture, but they have the apparatus." And that's true.

Believer: There was a period of time in the 1990s when queer writers were embraced by the mainstream publishing industry. Do you agree?

Schulman: It was caused by AIDS. AIDS made it impossible for people to deny that homosexuality exists. There were a couple of women editors—at Penguin, at Avon—there were a couple of lesbian editors who started publishing lesbian books in the mainstream. That went on from '85 to '92. In 1992, you started to get the niche marketing going on. That's when Barnes & Noble starts its gay and lesbian section, which is the worst thing that ever happened to us. That's when companies started hiring gay people to niche-market gay books to gay audiences. We were removed from mainstream literature. Then it was a self-fulfilling prophecy, because you could never get the sales. Instead of selling the books as American literature, they started to niche them as gay literature, and that killed it. That was the end of that little seven-year period. The end of that was the publication of *Bastard out of Carolina*, because it was a book that had no lesbian content but had an openly lesbian author. That was something that the industry could handle. But they could not promote and reward and have a great American success be a novel with a lesbian protagonist. The editors stopped being willing to publish those books. There was a time when seven to ten lesbian novels a year would be coming out of mainstream publishing houses. Now there are zero, or maybe two. It's the inability of the reading public to universalize to a lesbian protagonist. The industry has such a high ick factor that it's been unwilling to do what's necessary to help readers make that connection. But in Britain, lesbian writers are human beings. Their books are considered books, and regular people read them.

Believer: I want to ask you about your book *Ties That Bind: Familial Homophobia and Its Consequences*. What was its reception like?

Schulman: It got a very divided reception. In terms of regular queer people, I got two to six contacts per day from readers on Facebook, or email, or people leaving messages on my phone, letters, stopping me on the street; they were reading it in their church group in Iowa. I hadn't had that experience since *Rat Bohemia*, when people with AIDS would stop me on the street and say, "You really got it." To remember that you can actually write a book that can change people's lives is something I had forgotten. But I did not get a single review, or one mainstream review. It was this transformative book for all these people, and yet it doesn't exist.

Believer: Your novels are political because you're a political person, and your characters reflect that, but your fiction isn't didactic, and it doesn't seem as though the authorial voice has a political agenda. But when I read criticisms of your work, I feel that critics take your characters as political ideas. Yet books where characters talk about ideas that are considered politically mainstream are not critiqued this way. It reminded me of what the poet Sina Queyras tweeted a few months back: "Don't judge a book by your limitations." What do you think of that statement and how it might apply to your work?

Schulman: The problem is that novels that reinforce dominant culture values are considered to be neutral, but actually they are political. So they're like, why can't you be neutral like these really right-wing novels? That's the problem. In terms of reading reviews, I've only ever had one review that taught me something, and it was a negative review, and it was by Vivian Gornick; she's a genius, an older feminist woman. She reviewed *Rat Bohemia*. She said that these characters are not bohemians, because bohemians are refuseniks—they step out of their class position, but my characters had been thrown out. And I was like, You're right. That's it. All the other reviews, whether they rave, rave, rave, or hate, hate, hate, I never feel like they get it.

Believer: Do you feel that way when you talk to readers who give you feedback?

Schulman: Usually when people talk to me about the book, the benefit I get is I understand that it was meaningful to them, even if they hated it, because they were invested on some level. That is important information for me. But what I almost never get is that they read something that then gives them a deeper idea that they can bring back to me, and then we're actually in a dynamic conversation, so that I now think about something differently than I thought about it before. That almost never happens. The problem is that it takes a lot to really meet someone on the level of everything that they are offering in a novel. It's very easy to read superficially and to project.

Most people read just to find out about themselves, and it's interesting to me what readers have found out about themselves by reading my books, but it's not that helpful to me as a person. I also want to say that I've been very lucky that I've had a very high level of interaction with readers for my entire career, since 1984. I often walk into a room and there are people there who have read many of my books. Some of them I've aged with, as audiences or as readers. They're very engaged and very invested. If they hate something, they hate it, hate it, hate it. I've never had this experience of passive readers. I've gone to the readings of yuppie writers and I feel like their audience is completely unengaged. So I'm lucky. I'm writing for people who don't have any representation, and so they're happy to have something, and they want to interact with it.

Writer and Activist Sarah Schulman on *The Normal Heart*, Being Friends with Larry Kramer, and the Whitewashing of AIDS History

E. Alex Jung / 2014

From *Vulture*, June 1, 2014, https://www.vulture.com/2014/06/writer-sarah-schulman-on-the-normal-heart-larry-kramer.html. Reprinted with permission of VOX Media, LLC.

With *The Normal Heart*, Larry Kramer's largely autobiographical play turned recent HBO movie, it's impossible and maybe pointless to try to separate the personal from the political. The play's protagonist—and Kramer's stand-in—is Ned Weeks (Mark Ruffalo), the splenetic activist-writer who screamed at everyone who wouldn't listen, and even those who did. In many ways, it's a time capsule of the early years of the AIDS crisis when it was just a "gay cancer." The content reflected the reality: 1,112 dead and counting after just two years, indifference from the Koch and Reagan administrations, and a thoroughly freaked-out gay community that had just begun to feel the inklings of acceptance.

After the first production of the play in 1985 at the Public Theater, Kramer galvanized the gay community in the summer of 1987 with a speech, delivered at the LGBT Community Services Center, not unlike the kinds Ned delivers in the play. Its message was simple—if we do not fight, we will die. *Vulture* talked with playwright, novelist, and activist Sarah Schulman, who joined ACT UP a few months after its conception at that 1987 meeting, and developed a personal friendship with Kramer. A firebrand in her own right, she spoke about Larry Kramer's anger, the art of truth-telling, and how *The Normal Heart* is different from other AIDS narratives.

E. Alex Young: What was the political and cultural atmosphere like when *The Normal Heart* first premiered at The Public in 1985?

Sarah Schulman: I was very much in the underground at the time, so I can't tell you about official culture, but I was working as a reporter for subcultural newspapers like the *New York Native*. I was at City Hall covering the fact that we didn't have a gay rights bill, and then AIDS really began. In those early years I reported on the closing of the bathhouses, the first AIDS arrest, hearings at the City Council. It was a whirlwind of pain. Forty thousand people died of AIDS from 1981 to 1986. ACT UP was founded in 1987.

EAY: Like his persona Ned Weeks, Larry Kramer was a controversial figure in the AIDS movement, who seemed at once alienating and completely necessary.

SS: What made Larry different from everyone else was that he was a man with power who used his power and yelled at the powers that be. At that time, people who were really connected to the system did not use their access to help fight AIDS, and Larry did. That's a real huge difference between him and many other people of his class. I often feel that he's a very important part of the reason my friends who are alive are alive today. He never could come up with a strategy that worked. He couldn't get along with other people. He was dysfunctional in all those ways, but he used everything that he had. And many people who had more didn't do that.

I remember when Vito Russo died, which was a devastating death for the community. At the memorial service at Cooper Union, Larry's eulogy was, "We killed Vito. Don't you see that?" It was so off base. You had this room full of suffering, dying people who are fighting until their last breath, and he's saying, "We killed Vito." I remember friends of mine who had HIV saying, "I'm going to get a t-shirt saying, 'I killed Vito.'" There's all that kind of on an interpersonal level, as a member of a group—being out of touch.

EAY: What was the Broadway production of *The Normal Heart* like?

SS: When I went to see the show on Broadway, I really felt proud of him. The wonderful thing about *The Normal Heart* is that it does not give you this character of the heroic heterosexual who bravely overcomes her prejudices to help the poor, abandoned gay person who's all alone in the world. And that's the winning paradigm when you want Oscars and Pulitzer Prizes. This was a play that actually told the truth about how straight people behaved during the AIDS crisis, which was abominably. And it was not, like *Dallas Buyers Club*, the opposite of the truth. It was not straight people are the heroes of AIDS. They were destructive, abandoning, and indifferent. And Larry said that from the beginning, and he was right. So when I sat there on

Broadway and I saw him getting all of this praise for telling the truth, I know that that truth is true. I was very proud of him.

EAY: But it isn't simply about straight people as villains. He seems to have a lot of anger at the gay community for not fighting back.

SS: Yes, that's right. That's of course realistic, though. If ACT UP hadn't been formed, would the AIDS crisis have ever transformed? There always was this leadership that wanted to go along with things. And he resisted that. So his criticism of them is reasonable. But on the other hand, you understand why they were the way they were. Paul Popham [*Editor's note: The character Bruce Niles, played by Taylor Kitsch, is based on Paul Popham*], who I kind of remember, I believe he was a Green Beret. Some of these people came from really right-wing backgrounds. They weren't equipped because they hadn't ever been oppositional. Maybe because Larry was Jewish, maybe because he was kicked out of Yale, I don't know what the actual reasons are, but he already had the experience of seeing himself as oppositional.

EAY: Why do you think it took so long for a film to be made?

SS: Well the film happened because of the success of the Broadway show, right? Why did that take so long? I don't know. But you know we're so far behind. I've been at this for a really long time and when you have an idea that's an original idea, you usually are misunderstood, because they confuse familiarity with quality. So then you have to wait, sometimes decades until your original idea is now the status quo. Either they remember that you had it in the first place or they wait for someone else to come along and have it again. And then it gets praised. That's the normal cycle.

EAY: What was the difference between what Larry Kramer was trying to do with his plays versus his political screeds and speeches?

SS: I guess *The Normal Heart* is personal. And some of his political writing, his analogies between AIDS and the Holocaust didn't work; that was not a successful intellectual venture. I think he's a better feeler than he is a thinker. I've interviewed 168 surviving members of ACT UP New York for the ACT UP Oral History Project and almost everyone who talks about him talks about him the same way. They're all annoyed with him on some level and yet they love him. He enrages them, but they all know what he's done for them.

EAY: Returning to the play, Kramer has said that formal aesthetic concerns are not important to him. Do you think that's true?

SS: It's possible. You could compare it to *Angels in America*, which has this very ornamented theatricality. For many people, that is the most important element of the play and Larry doesn't have that. But the content of *Angels in America* is that there's a gay man who abandons his lover when he has AIDS. That almost never happened in real life. And then he has the Reaganite Mormon who heroically takes the poor, abandoned gay man to the emergency room because there's no gay people there to help him. That's the opposite of the truth. So you have people who are impressed by it, formally, but there's very little discussion of what it's actually saying. I remember feeling this at the time, was that what it was describing was not the truth. The truth was that people with AIDS were abandoned by their families and they joined together and they forced this country to change against its will. That's not the story that the dominant culture wanted to hear. That's Larry's story. It's not encased in something that engages or perhaps distracts.

But you know one of the things in American theater is that the meaning and values of the work [are] almost never discussed, whether it's condemned or praised. Rarely do people say, what does this play stand for? And when we look at what *The Normal Heart* stands for, it really holds up.

EAY: Do you feel like we need a Larry Kramer now in the queer community?

SS: Who's we? Now we're in the homonationalist era. Now we're at the era of the reconciliation of the white race through gay marriage and gay family and gay rights. And gay people who have certain kinds of privileges whether they're white or citizens or HIV negative allying themselves to the state and using the state apparatus that separates them from other people. This is where we are now. But there is no "we." It's not the same "we" that it was at that era or that time.

EAY: Well, I would question whether it ever was, even then.

SS: Well, ACT UP was successful because it had all these different kinds of people and it allowed all different kinds of people no matter what their background to act in a way that made sense individually. It did not try to control. There was no attempt to homogenize people's behavior and that's why it was a successful movement.

EAY: What did you think of *How to Survive a Plague*? There seemed to be a certain whitewashing of history going on.

SS: Well, we call it "The Five White People Who Saved the World"—that's our nickname for it. And those white people are very busy, because apparently they're always saving everything all the time. Everywhere you go, you see them.

Jim Hubbard, the director of *United in Anger: A History of ACT UP*, and David France did a public debate. It was cosponsored by Visual AIDS and you can watch it on YouTube and it's really, really fascinating. At one point they open up for questions and the first question to David is: Why do you have no women or people of color in the film? And he says, well, I wanted to focus on wealthy white men because they had the time to devote to activism. Now as a person who has interviewed 168 surviving members of ACT UP New York, I can tell you that's not historically correct. People in ACT UP gave their entire lives to ACT UP. All different kinds of people from every class and background would report in our interviews that they were at ACT UP five nights a week, that their entire life was ACT UP. And that had nothing to do with how much money you had. And the second thing he said was that these men went to good universities and so they were able to understand the science. That is absurd. The audience almost started laughing. One of the best experts on the science of AIDS in ACT UP was Garance Franke-Ruta, who was nineteen. We all sat there and realized that this man knows nothing about ACT UP.

EAY: And yet France's documentary was widely praised and even nominated for an Academy Award in 2013.

SS: Because it does the same thing that *Philadelphia* does: It makes the dominant culture comfortable. It gives them heroes that look like them that they can identify with. That's the story that they want. In *Philadelphia*, the straight lawyer heroically overcomes his prejudice to help the poor gay man. Why Tom Hanks's character didn't just get a gay lawyer is something I never understood about that movie. It had this bizarre conceit, but that's what straight people want. Now we have this whiteness that is uniting gay people, especially gay men, with the rest of the white race. This is pervasive, now we see that straight people can identify with these white gay protagonists, it made them the heroes. That's why they like it. It doesn't matter that it wasn't true.

Book Brahmin: Sarah Schulman

Shelf Awareness / 2016

From shelf-awareness.com, March 30, 2016. Reprinted with permission of *Shelf Awareness* and Robin Lenz.

Sarah Schulman is a novelist, playwright, screenwriter, nonfiction writer, AIDS historian and journalist. She is Distinguished Professor of the Humanities at the City University of New York, College of Staten Island, a fellow at the New York Institute for the Humanities at New York University, on the advisory board of Jewish Voice for Peace and faculty adviser to Students for Justice in Palestine. Schulman is cofounder of the ACT UP Oral History Project and MIX NYC Queer Experimental Film Festival. *The Cosmopolitans* (Feminist Press, March 15, 2016) is her tenth novel, and seventeenth book.

Shelf Awareness: On your nightstand now.

Sarah Schulman: *Queer Activism in India: A Story in the Anthropology of Ethics* by Naisargi Dave; *Voyage of the Sable Venus and Other Poems* by Robin Coste Lewis; *Ma mère rit* by Chantal Akerman; *Nochita* by Dia Felix; *The Odd Woman and the City* by Vivian Gornick; and *Agnes Martin: Her Life and Art* by Nancy Princenthal.

SA: Favorite book when you were a child.

SS: *Goodnight Moon* by Margaret Wise Brown, *Harriet the Spy* by Louise Fitzhugh, *The Pushcart War* by Jean Merrill, *The Diary of a Young Girl* by Anne Frank.

I think the important influences here come from the learned knowledge that girls could be writers, that urban life was a reasonable subject for literature and that there is a beauty in repetition. *Goodnight, moon. Goodnight, red balloon.*

SA: Your top five authors.

SS: Carson McCullers—I have spent most of my adult life thinking about Carson McCullers. In 2002, I had a play produced at Playwrights Horizons,

Carson McCullers, and have since written a film, *Lonely Hunter*, and am now working on a novel in which she appears. I have read everything she has written that I could get my hands on, including juvenilia, and most of what has been written about her. The mystery and allure of McCullers is how a young white woman from segregated Georgia, could—at age twenty-three—publish a book that Richard Wright could call the first book by a white writer with fully realized Black characters. She had an incredible ability to inhabit any kind of person: a Filipino gay man, a dwarf, a Jewish gay deaf mute. How did she do it? The question is a mesmerizing one.

Jean Genet was the first writer on romance that I believed. I was handed his book *Funeral Rites* in high school by a girl who said, "Here, you're a romantic," and have been compelled towards his work ever since. My most recent investigation was a piece called "Jean Genet in Palestine," which will appear in a new anthology honoring Edmund White.

Rabih Alameddine is the most exciting novelist in my life. His first novel *Koolaids: The Art of War*, which juxtaposes the AIDS crisis with the Lebanese Civil War, is one of the most successful AIDS novels to date. The formal breaks artfully replicate the emotionality of that period and that context.

Claudia Rankine, of course, is a writer who has the community's trust.

And I read and am enriched by all my friends who inspire me.

SA: Book you're an evangelist for.

SS: *I, the Divine* by Rabih Alameddine. Anyone who wants to be a better writer should read this book.

SA: Book you've bought for the cover.

SS: *Tripmaster Monkey: His Fake Book* by Maxine Hong Kingston, and I loved it.

SA: Book that changed your life.

SS: Most recent book to change my life is John Keene's *Counternarratives*. It is a masterful work, twenty years in the making, that reveals the inability of conventional narrative structure to contain the individual and collective experience of slavery over time and place.

SA: Favorite line from a book.

SS: "It happened that green and crazy summer"—from *The Member of the Wedding* by Carson McCullers.

SA: Five books you'll never part with.

SS: *Funeral Rites* by Jean Genet, *The Ballad of the Sad Café* by Carson McCullers, *Citizen: An American Lyric* by Claudia Rankine, *Visions of Cody* by Jack Kerouac, and "The Transformation of Silence into Language and Action" by Audre Lorde.

SA: Book you most want to read again for the first time.

SS: *Wide Sargasso Sea* by Jean Rhys. This author wrote four novels in the 1920s, then drank for some decades, only to produce her great work in the 1960s, when many readers thought she was dead. I want to understand that surprise of holding a story as long as one can, until it lives on its own.

SA: Not-yet-published books that you are looking forward to.

SS: Because I live in the world of writers, I often know what my favorites are working on long before the books are published or even fully written. In the near and long future, I am looking forward to: Tracie Morris's forthcoming experimental dialogues with five artists, Rabih's book about AIDS and Tayari Jones's new novel imagining real autonomy for Black women, which are still being written. I am holding a place in my heart for many nonfiction books: the long-awaited in-progress biographies of Lorraine Hansberry, Kathy Acker and Muriel Rukeyser; Matt Brim's *Poor Queer Theory*, which is half written. Far in the future: Nan Alamilla Boyd's *History of Tourism in San Francisco* and Susan Stryker's *Transgender History*. Anything from Claudia Rankine and Martha Hodes. Plus all my students everywhere and the life-changing books I have yet to imagine.

Sarah Schulman on Her Latest Provocations

Chris Freeman / 2016

From the *Gay & Lesbian Review Worldwide*, July/August 2016. Reprinted with permission.

I first encountered Sarah Schulman in January 1996, when she was a speaker at "Literature in the Age of AIDS" in Key West. That was a world ago. We met again a couple of years later at UNC-Asheville, where she was beginning to articulate her ideas about "familial homophobia," the central idea in her remarkable book *Ties That Bind*. Schulman has spent her whole adult life as a journalist, novelist, playwright, and activist. In 2016, she has two new books, a novel called *The Cosmopolitans*, which came out in the spring, and the powerful nonfiction book *Conflict Is Not Abuse*, due out October. Hugh Ryan recently wrote a long retrospective piece on Schulman's body of work for the *Los Angeles Review of Books*. In assessing the power of her voice, he observed that Schulman "places a high premium on accountability, responsibility, and consistency, and it shows in the way she chases an idea from book to book, from nonfiction to fiction and back again." Ryan's insight is spot on. Schulman is a public intellectual, an artist, an idea maker; she does not shy away from controversy and does not seek the spotlight. For me, her integrity as an artist and a citizen makes her a singular presence in American (queer) culture.

Chris Freeman: You are a distinguished professor, an author, an activist, but you had an unconventional education for someone in your professional position.

Sarah Schulman: I had an excellent public-school education at Hunter High School, which was at the time a school for smart girls. Elena Kagan was a year behind me, but we were in student government together. Then I went to the University of Chicago, where I was a terrible student. I dropped out. After Chicago, I went to Hunter College, where Audre Lorde was my teacher, and I finally got my BA from Empire State College. But at Chicago, I had a class on nineteenth-century French realism. Balzac's novel *Cousin Bette* stuck with me all these years, and it showed up again for me in 2003 in a play called *The Burning Deck* that I wrote for the La Jolla Playhouse. The play was expanded into *The Cosmopolitans*.

CF: While you've been an artist and writer since your twenties, it looks to me as if you've been an activist all your life.

SS: I came back to New York in 1979, and two important things happened around that time. After leaving Chicago, I went to Europe (with my student loan money) and was involved with an illegal abortion situation, not for myself, but for a friend. When I came back to the United States, the Hyde Amendment had just passed, which attempted to limit women's rights to abortions, so I got involved in fighting that immediately. I became a member of CARASA (Committee for Abortion Rights and Against Sterilization Abuse). I was part of a protest at Congress, a direct action. With the Women's Liberation Zap Action Brigade, I disrupted a congressional antiabortion hearing and was charged with "disruption of Congress." That is the first time I got arrested. CARASA didn't like that strategy, and that political difference over direct action was soon followed by other conflicts that resulted in a lesbian purge.

CF: A strange parallel to a decade earlier when the lesbians were kicked out of NOW.

SS: Yes, exactly. And this coincided with my work for *Womanews*, a new feminist paper. I covered the radical right (what would become the Tea Party) and the antiabortion movement for them.

CF: Is that where your career as a journalist really started?

SS: Yes. I wrote for *Womanews*, *Gay Community News*, and *The Guardian*, a hundred-year-old Marxist paper out of New York, and *The Native*. They're all movement publications: *GCN* was left-wing gay men and women; *The Native* was for gay men; *The Guardian* was lefty and almost antigay; and *Womanews* was a feminist paper for gay and straight women. I'm still a journalist. I published a piece in *Slate* recently on HIV criminalization.

CF: You started covering AIDS early on.

SS: I did a piece for *The Native* about the first AIDS case in the Soviet Union in the early 1980s. We had no concept of AIDS as global. That was my first HIV piece. I was a City Hall reporter for *The Native*. Ed Koch was mayor, and I used to go to meetings and press conferences to ask about when we were finally going to have a gay rights bill. And then AIDS started, so I was on that beat already. I covered the closing of the bathhouses for *The Native* too. The fact that I was assigned to this story reveals how chaotic coverage was. After all, I was not allowed in the bathhouses. Reporters were dying. It was hard to understand what the stories actually were.

CF: You also wrote about AIDS for the *Village Voice*.

SS: The *Voice* had two editors who covered AIDS, Robert Massa and Richard Goldstein. Goldstein wrote long, personal pieces; Massa had AIDS and wanted to cover it in a much broader context. He was my real editor, but he was dying. I did the first story on women's exclusion from drug trials. I had to go to Robert's apartment when we worked; he was that sick. He died when I was in the middle of a story about pediatric AIDS. I was writing on AIDS in a social context. Goldstein was not interested in these issues. The piece I wrote about double-blind placebo studies with infants and HIV was not something Goldstein wanted to run, so I published it in *Womanews*. After that, I was no longer part of the *Voice*. I pitched twelve ideas to *The Nation*—and I wrote the first story ever on AIDS and homeless people. It appealed to them in part because it was a class or an economic story, not a "gay" story. So AIDS and social justice is something I have focused on for more than thirty years, as a writer and an activist. I'm still on that beat. My new book, *Conflict Is Not Abuse*, has a huge section on HIV criminalization.

CF: Your career as an artist was also beginning to gain traction at the same time.

SS: My first novel, *The Sophie Horowitz Story*, came out in 1984, from Naiad, a lesbian press run by Barbara Grier, who had been the book editor at *The Ladder* for the Daughters of Bilitis. I had about sixty rejections. I got letters saying that it was so funny, but if only the character weren't a lesbian. My girlfriend's other girlfriend was a temp at Scribner's, and she sent my manuscript on their letterhead, which got the attention of Naiad. They took it, but they didn't really know what to do with a Jewish novel. The drawing of Sophie on the cover made her look Black. The cover copy said, "Sophie is up to her Jewish earlobes in murder and intrigue." It was highly racialized. The book was read, though. It represented a generational shift; I was part of a generation of lesbian writers who had never been in the closet. So, whereas most previous lesbian literature was a dance between popular culture and a kind of lesbian subculture, the writers of my generation didn't write that way. For us, lesbians were part of popular culture. So I wrote a detective novel with a lesbian protagonist. Then in 1986, I wrote a book called *Girls, Visions and Everything*, which was published by Seal Press. In it, I was responding to the literature of Beat culture in the East

Village in [the] 1960s, but with an eighties lesbian spin. The next year, ACT UP was founded and I became part of it, and that same year Jim Hubbard and I founded MIX, the New York Queer Experimental Film Festival. So experimental film, activism, and writing were all part of what I was doing.

CF: In a sense your writing career in the 1980s and '90s was part of the rise, the peak, and the splintering of publishing, both in terms of gay books and of how publishing worked.

SS: Absolutely. My novel *After Dolores* was published by Dutton in 1988 and was reviewed, by a straight man, in the *New York Times*. It was a rave review; it was life changing, and I turned thirty that year. This was before niche marketing. The book was translated into eight languages. Mainstream publishers began to acquire lesbian titles; there was a big discussion at the time about big publishing houses versus women's presses for lesbian books.

CF: Didn't Dutton publish Dorothy Allison's *Bastard out of Carolina* in 1992?

SS: Yes, and a lot happened in the five or so years between *After Dolores* and *Bastard*. Mainly, AIDS, which created a visibility for gay things. The first OutWrite conference was in 1990; queer writing was growing in popularity. Allison's novel created a quandary for the publishing industry. She was an out lesbian, but her novel did not have lesbian content. This was new. Thus developed a two-tiered marketing program. *Bastard* was sold as "general fiction," while people like me became part of "lesbian fiction." This is when Barnes & Noble started having a "gay and lesbian" section. The review I got a few years earlier in the *New York Times* would never really happen again, because we were all competing for the very few niched "lesbian" spots in mainstream coverage.

CF: The OutWrite conferences are important documents of this incredible time in queer life and publishing. There is footage on YouTube of you at the San Francisco conference back in 1990, on a panel called "AIDS and the Responsibility of the Writer," with Essex Hemphill, John Preston, Pat Califia, and Susan Griffin. It is stunning to watch this, seeing each of you in the first decade of the epidemic trying to make sense of it. You talked about your then-new novel, *People in Trouble*. You said, "I identified for myself the category of 'witness fiction.' . . . In writing about something of this enormity, when it surrounds you, it leaves those of us who write about AIDS no possibility of objectivity; nor can there be any conclusiveness, since the crisis around us changes daily. I knew that what I was writing would already be history when it was published." It is astonishing to watch and listen to this "of the moment" conversation from today's perspective.

SS: That was the opening plenary of the conference. Essex and John died not too long after that. People were dying right in front of us. I remember Craig Harris, a Black writer, who could barely stand up and was dripping with sweat. Jim Hubbard and I, in working on the ACT UP Oral History Project, have realized that we as a community have been good at documenting and writing about the heroism of AIDS, but not about the suffering. We have not been able to convey the depth of the suffering.

CF: Some of your AIDS-related writing was published in *My American History: Lesbian and Gay Life during the Reagan/Bush Years* (1994).

SS: Yes, and that is my first book of nonfiction. It is my journalism from before AIDS, through the epicenter of the crisis. It is about the transformation as I started to understand what was happening. I'm one of the few people who've been writing about AIDS from the beginning. It is an enduring relationship for me. With the ACT UP Oral History Project, I've conducted 187 long-form interviews with ACT UP members over the past fifteen years. Jim Hubbard and I now know more cumulatively about ACT UP than anybody.

CF: In 1998, your talk at the literature conference at the University of North Carolina, Asheville was about "familial homophobia," something you've spent more than a decade writing and thinking about. This work culminated in *Ties That Bind* (2009). I think this is such an important part of your legacy.

SS: I started using first person in *My American History*, and that was important. Never forget that I'm not an academic. Nobody wanted to publish *Ties That Bind*. This happens with a lot of my work. It was the very first book to identify familial homophobia. I had to coin that term, because gay people just called it "it."

CF: How do you approach writing nonfiction? Is it different from fiction for you?

SS: I never write about an ongoing conversation. That is to say, every nonfiction book I write is to initiate a conversation. Sometimes it works, sometimes it doesn't. For example, *Ties That Bind* has not been as widely read as *Gentrification of the Mind*, but I believe *Ties* should have been published by a mainstream publisher. When you are the first person to present an idea, it is not easy to get published. Gatekeepers don't recognize it as what it is: new knowledge.

CF: *Gentrification of the Mind* is a groundbreaking, insightful book. It helps us understand modern cities, modern ways of thinking and living. You are a kind of case study of urban life: your life for half a century in New York is a record of these cultural shifts. First, where did you get that title?

SS: I gave a talk at the New School in the 1990s with that title, and I kept it. It was kind of a weird talk; basically, I was noticing that people were being mean everywhere. I wanted to know why. The culture was homogenizing. One thing I cited in the original talk was that, in the earlier years, I could call any lesbian, and she'd call me back. I remember a lesbian dance critic named Jennifer Dunning at the *New York Times*. I called her because two gay people were burned to death in Oregon as part of the antigay initiative there. I wanted the *Times* to cover it; she called me back. I told her what had happened and she did the internal stuff and got it covered. But younger lesbians wouldn't call me back. Why? Because they had been gentrified. They have rights and privileges that we had not had. They took it for granted, but they theorized it as their own personal triumph, rather than as something that my generation had fought for and won. They didn't understand why they had the power they had.

CF: I think *Gentrification* is such a comprehensive book. It's small but powerful, sort of thesis driven.

SS: I'm realizing that my theme for my entire body of work is, "Why are people mean?" It's the subject of my new nonfiction book, too.

CF: You are doing a genealogy of meanness. Tell me about what you are taking on in that new project.

SS: It's called *Conflict Is Not Abuse: Overstating Harm, Community Responsibility, and the Duty of Repair*. It's about three realms where I feel that conflict is misrepresented as abuse, through the overstatement of harm: the interpersonal realm, the criminalization of HIV, and Israel/Palestine. I define conflict as "power struggle" and abuse as "power over." My thesis is that when we deny our participation in creating conflict, and instead claim that we are victims of abuse, the power of the state is enhanced.

CF: Like calling the police instead of having a conversation with someone.

SS: Yes, and people get killed. So with the criminalization of HIV, for instance, these laws encourage people to call the police on someone who didn't disclose their HIV status, regardless of their health, viral load, or whatever. For the past thirty years, the HIV-negative person has been seen as being responsible for that status and for maintaining it; with criminalization, the HIV-positive person becomes the "abuser," while the negative person is now the person who has been criminally wronged. It is a state apparatus exploiting a new social trend of us not taking personal responsibility for our role in situations of conflict. Or, to give a different example,

New York City has two hundred thousand cases of domestic violence, so when someone overreacts to conflict, claiming abuse when it is not abuse, they redirect resources away from those who most need them. The book's final example is an analysis of the rhetoric surrounding the 2014 Israeli war on Gaza. Again, we see the exteriorizing of interior anxiety, negative group loyalty, the refusal to face one's own role in creating conflict: all these elements that the book articulates converge on the murder of over two thousand people in Gaza. I show that the same tropes an individual uses to claim "abuse" because they misunderstood or were made uncomfortable by an email, become the tools of government propaganda, that there is a direct relationship between the intimate refusal of accountability to the nationalistic projection. If we shun, cold-shoulder or bully the people we know because they say something or exhibit difference in a way that makes us uncomfortable, how are we going to be able to make peace or welcome refugees, or win justice? These two actions are antithetical.

CF: The final section of the book brings up your role as an outspoken critic of Israel. You've taken a lot of criticism and even had hatred and threats directed at you for being so vocal in your criticism of Israel.

SS: The truth is, I'm a tenured professor, so I haven't had a lot of fear about my job security. Recently, though, I was falsely accused of anti-Semitism, and I did fear for my job when that happened. But I've never felt much at risk. Other people, particularly Arab professors like Steven Salaita at the University of Illinois, who lost his job because of his position on Palestine, are in far more jeopardy than I am.

CF: I suppose your work on conflict situates you to be quite willing to engage in strenuous debate around these controversial issues.

SS: I talk to people constantly whom I disagree with about Israel. I feel that it's my responsibility to do that. The occupation is being carried out in my name on two grounds: because I'm Jewish and American. When I talk to really extremist people on this issue, it becomes immediately clear that they are grossly uninformed. Usually they have never had real experiences with Palestinians and have not listened to what they have to say about their own experiences. In the United States, this information is not passively acquired.

CF: I'm guessing this is another book that was hard for you to publish.

SS: Academic presses were concerned that because I don't have advanced credentials, I would not be able to pass editorial review boards. I approach nonfiction as an artist. My books are not about "proof." You don't come out of a play and say, "That play was right!" You say, "that play revealed human contradictions." My method is to offer a lot of ideas, and readers become interactive, in this way producing new knowledge. As far as commercial publishing goes, in the United States, Palestine cannot be used as an example for a larger argument. It is so stigmatized and underdiscussed that it can only be its own subject. People are so ignorant, they have so little access to good information, that they don't have the context to see how Palestine could be an example of something other than itself. The book wound up with Arsenal, a Canadian press, which seems fitting since HIV criminalization is happening in Canada. But will anyone in the US pay attention to it? We will see.

CF: Your other new book in 2016 is a novel, *The Cosmopolitans*, set in Greenwich Village in 1958. We follow a woman, Bette, who is fifty, from Ohio, and she has a kind of small life in New York. She has not had feminism to help her. Her best friend and neighbor is Earl, a Black, gay actor, whose life is more dramatic than hers. The novel has an intelligence and a sincerity to it. It's a lovely but disturbing book. We find out that the building where they live is the building on 10th Street where you spent some years growing up. That is a fascinating crossing between fiction and autobiography.

SS: This is all very layered, as is the book. It took me thirteen years to write; I started it when I was forty-four and finished it when I was fifty-seven. It's a look back at my urban origins, but also it's a portrait of pregentrification New York. I wanted to evoke the New York that was a refuge for people from uncomprehending backgrounds. The performance artist Penny Arcade has this joke about how we all left home and came to New York to get away from the most popular kids in school, and now, with gentrification, they've all moved to New York. It is the very people who couldn't survive in their small towns who made New York a center for the production of ideas for the world, the very people who are getting squeezed out now. The novel shows neighbors and relationships, what apartment living produced; suburbanization privatized these human relations. The literary look back is to Balzac's novel *Cousin Bette*, which, as I mentioned earlier, I studied at the University of Chicago in a class on nineteenth-century French realism. In Balzac's novel, a spinster is betrayed by her family and wants to get revenge. So, she destroys everybody and everything, and in the end she wins. And, also, from the late fifties, early sixties is James Baldwin's *Another Country*—Black and white and gay and straight—on these same streets, but the women in the book are not real people. Balzac, Baldwin, and 1950s kitchen sink realism are all called "real," but how can that be so? The artist in me was intrigued.

CF: These ideas coalesced for you over more than a decade, and they called back over your whole life.

SS: Yes, and then in 2003 a stage actress, Roberta Maxwell, asked me to write a play for her at the La Jolla Playhouse. *Cousin Bette* seemed like a great fit for that project. I decided to update it. It was in a program that included public readings and feedback, but the play, which was called *The Burning Deck*, a line from Elizabeth Bishop, was never actually performed. I worked with an actress named Diane Venora, who was the last woman to play Hamlet. In fact, in her career, she is the only actor in history to have played Ophelia, Gertrude, and Hamlet. Joe Papp directed her in *Hamlet*. I spent four weeks with her on this project. The actor Mark Lonnie Smith played Earl. So I saw these characters move around. But it was clear that it wasn't going to get produced, because the people in charge, the ones who run theaters, don't understand these kinds of relationships of the powerless, where there are no white male protagonists, where it's neither a "Black" play nor a "white" one.

CF: So that's maybe why the novel is structured as Act One, Intermission, and Act Two.

SS: Right, and Act Two is the revenge plot. A person has been transformed by having been falsely accused; she has a new tool, marketing, that provides her with power.

CF: Bette has Valerie, a first-generation ad executive, as a female ally.

SS: Well, kind of, but to me, women who went into advertising in the 1950s and sixties are sort of like the women who became psychoanalysts fifty years earlier. New fields have room for women; old fields do not. But the irony of women in advertising is that they ended up making a lot of money and getting a lot of autonomy, but at the expense of women in general. Advertising is the enemy of women. The woman who came up with the campaigns "If I have one life to live, let me live it as a blonde" and "Blondes have more fun" was a Jewish brunette contributing to white supremacy. So you get this kind of "power feminism" which came at a high cost for women, though not for individual women.

CF: In your novel, there is a lot of conflict. What fiction allows you to do is show it resolved or not resolved. You are essentially getting to work some of these issues out with these characters. Your nonfiction writing is helping you write your fiction, in that way. For me, you are an idea writer, a public intellectual, albeit for what is now a small public.

SS: I'm a subcultural public intellectual. I'm not on NPR, for example.

CF: I learned a lot from *The Cosmopolitans*—about community, about capitalism and advertising, about women's lives, and about gay lives. It is a kind of social critique.

SS: Yes, Earl and Bette are out there on their own, without the benefit of feminism, the gay rights movement, or the Black Power movement. The idea of a community thinking out loud about their own condition has not yet occurred. They had to figure it out themselves.

CF: This novel couldn't be set ten years later. It captures that "before" moment.

SS: It couldn't be set even five years later. After the JFK assassination, everything started to shift quickly. Eisenhower is president in this book.

CF: So now I am thinking about today. The kind of community you depict in *The Cosmopolitans* will never happen again, not in the contemporary cities. So what do we have now? Facebook? You and I are Facebook friends, and you are quite active on it. Is that a new form of community making, community building in the twenty-first century?

SS: For me, personally, Facebook is very, very rich. I've gotten so much out of it on so many levels. The international information is extraordinary. In a matter of seconds, I can find things out from all over the world, and not from news media. So that's amazing. But also, I've been able to put out ideas and get many, many responses. *Conflict Is Not Abuse* is a book that I basically wrote using Facebook. I'd put out a thought and get so many suggestions and responses. It is humanizing, seeing people on vacation, or hearing their frustrations, whatever. A lot of people don't use Facebook and can be self-righteous about that, but for me, it has helped me see other people, specific people, more multidimensionally, and they can see me that way too.

CF: I have to say I agree with you. I've posted, for example, about my father's death and have been incredibly moved by the hundreds of responses. There's humanity there.

SS: Yes, but you also have to practice restraint. The cruelty between the Hillary and Bernie people has been outrageous, but I don't delete or block that stuff, because it's part of what I'm working on. The pro-Israel crazy people do horrible things to me—they alter my Wikipedia page, they post vicious things—but what I have realized is that if I just let them express their opinions and move on, nothing terrible happens. I'm not diminished in any way. Only when I get on their level do I get diminished. My phone number is listed. I know many writers of all levels of success who have unlisted their numbers, as if they think of themselves in a constant state of siege. But because I'm accessible, there's no anxiety around me. Anyone who wants to talk to me can, so no one is desperate to talk to me. We can just communicate, we can reformulate a relationship.

Close Encounters: Sarah Schulman with Jarrett Earnest

Jarrett Earnest / 2016

From the *Brooklyn Rail*, December 6, 2016. Reprinted with permission.

The novelist, playwright, and critic Sarah Schulman has been chronicling bohemian life in the East Village since the late 1970s. Her work as participant and chronicler of ACT UP is the stuff of queer legend, as is her cofounding of MIX NYC, the NY Queer Experimental Film Festival in 1987 that is going into its thirtieth year. Her newest book, *Conflict Is Not Abuse*, is aimed at disentangling "conflict," as a *Power Struggle*, from "abuse," which is *Power Over*. The difference, she argues, is that if we work together to recognize our complicity in conflicts we can resolve them before they spiral out of control. We met in her apartment on 9th Street on the eve of the presidential election.

Jarrett Earnest: The occasion of our conversation is your new book, *Conflict Is Not Abuse*, but I wanted to talk with you about the larger trajectory of your writing. because there is an unbroken river of thought in your nonfiction that goes from *Stagestruck* (1998) to *Ties That Bind* (2009) through *The Gentrification of the Mind* (2012) and *Israel/Palestine and the Queer International* (2012) and culminates in this new book. Something I wondered about was the context of your upbringing in a Jewish family in New York City. Some things about this book that have been touchy relate to "victimhood" and I'm wondering how your relationship to that discourse was shaped by growing up in the aftermath of the Holocaust.

Sarah Schulman: My family was truly victimized. My grandmother who lived with us had two brothers and two sisters exterminated by the Nazis, and my grandfather's sister was murdered by Nazis—this was very close. I was born thirteen years after the end of the Holocaust. It was very real to me.

Earnest: In your bio at the back of *Conflict Is Not Abuse* you cite two books that made you want to be a writer: *The Diary of Anne Frank* (1947) and *Harriet the Spy* (1964). Positioning *The Diary of Anne Frank* at the beginning of your relationship to being an artist makes me think that your Jewish identity was intimately connected with it.

Schulman: I knew about the Holocaust since I was born. There was never a time I didn't know about it. I was from a generation where the kids sat there while the parents talked. So of course it's very influential in everything I do—it's my number one influence.

Earnest: When in your adolescence were you first conscious of being attracted to women?

Schulman: I don't know the answer to that. I was in elementary school in 1962—this is before feminism, so keep that in mind—and our nursery schoolteacher was getting married and was marriage-crazy so she organized the class into a mass wedding. Everyone had to line up boy-girl and march down the aisle, but I refused and said that I would be the photographer and I ran around the wedding holding my hands as though I were holding a Kodak Instamatic snapping fake photographs—that is my coming out right there. My father grew up in Elizabeth, New Jersey, which was a poor, gray town. He came from one of those Jewish families that had a store they lived over. He had two best friends from that town, and one of them broke up with his wife and came and lived with us in our apartment. His kid came to visit him in our house and she told me that when she grew up she wanted to be a lesbian. That is the first time I heard that word.

Earnest: How old were you?

Schulman: Six or seven. But it wasn't a word that was bandied about, the way it is today. I think one of the really key events around this was when I was at the University of Chicago, where I went and dropped out before going to Hunter College. At the University of Chicago it was almost completely forbidden to discuss homosexuality in the classroom. They had a "Great Books" curriculum, which was a required program that ended with Marx, Freud, and Weber—this was before poststructuralism. We weren't allowed to study anything by women. There was only one thing in the whole of "Great Books" by a woman and that was Sappho in the pre-Socratics. So we never read primary texts by women. We took courses like "Images of Women in French Literature," where we read *Madame Bovary*, *Nana*, and all these books by men. I took that class, and once when Colette was mentioned I raised my hand and said, *wasn't Colette a lesbian?* And the teacher replied, *if a writer is a lesbian or not is as important as if she's right-handed* *or left-handed*. Now, I'm sitting there as a future lesbian writer thinking, *I'm not sure but don't think that's right!*

Earnest: When were you introduced to lesbian culture?

Schulman: At that time there were two levels of public high schools—district school and magnet schools. If you were a good student you could go to the magnet school, and they were gender-segregated: Hunter was for girls and Stuyvesant was for boys. Audre Lorde and Cynthia Nixon went to Hunter, for example, and I went there at the same time as Elena Kagan. I started in 1971, the year abortion became legal in New York City before *Roe v. Wade* made it national in 1973. So here I am in a school full of girls; the women's movement was exploding and there was a lot of gay stuff—there were girls who were couples and we knew who they were. There were consciousness-raising groups. Someone wrote "Gay Liberation Come Out" on the wall of my school—I was exposed to all of that.

But even younger, I think when I was eight or nine, there was a gay-bar raid and a guy was arrested who was Argentinian who didn't have a green card. They took him into the police station on 12th Street and he tried to escape and jumped out the window and was impaled on the fence. I lived on 10th Street, and I knew about that. So I had knowledge of gay things.

Earnest: When did you connect those two parts of your life, your writing life and lesbian identity?

Schulman: Probably from the beginning. For example, *The Diary of Anne Frank* had lesbian content that the father censored out, so I probably sensed something. Similarly *Harriet the Spy* was written by a lesbian, Louise Fitzhugh. She was part of a circle around Trude Heller, who was Carmen McRae's lover, and who owned a jazz club on 11th Street, which included people like Marijane Meaker, who wrote lesbian pulp novels under the name Vin Packer and had an affair with Patricia Highsmith. There was this whole circle of lesbian writers in the West Village that Louise Fitzhugh was a part of. I'm sure both of those books had huge lesbian subtexts.

Earnest: One of the things I thought was the most important about *Conflict Is Not Abuse* connects to our contemporary moment, where people displace conflict through various means. One is through media where you don't have direct personal interaction, or by deferring to institutional structures that intervene, whether that is a school administration or on up to the state. How [do] you see conflict working differently now than twenty years ago?

Schulman: In the book I give the history of the transformation of the feminist movement against male violence, and I really try and show that it is post-Reagan where we start seeing the constant message that police should be the arbiters of human relationships. That began the bureaucratizing and professionalizing of social services so that they become part of the government, eliminating the grassroots sector the community was providing. You also get the emergence of corporate television shows like *Law & Order* showing us that there is one perpetrator who is evil, there is one victim who is innocent, and the answer is the police. It's now been thirty-six years that we've been told that police are the appropriate arbiters of relationship conflict, and that is not true—it's true for *abuse*, perhaps, but for conflict it is absolutely not true.

Earnest: I'm wondering if it's more common to avoid having actual conflicts in person, which makes the conversation urgent and immediate. What does it mean, then, to disagree as human beings?

Schulman: We've conflated taking responsibility with having something be your *fault*. So, for example, if someone wants their partner to leave and they won't, it now escalates to *if you don't do it right now, then I'm calling the police*, then they call the police. What if the community around those people, friends, neighbors, and families, instead said, *we're going to come over and find out what's going on*. What would be revealed if they stayed? What do you think the problem is? What are the alternatives to calling the police? To me, that intervention is what loyalty really is. That means we allow people to say *I overreacted* without being punished.

Earnest: How do you understand the construction of community in this context?

Schulman: It's whatever groups you belong to. I've lived in this apartment building since 1979 and there are a few people I've lived with this entire time. We have seen each other through all kinds of shit—horrible breakups, overdoses—and there's a sense of community that you live in. So that's one kind of community. For some people it's their family, or friends, or religious categories; a lot of us are in cliques; some of us have work colleagues. There are all kinds of witnesses to our lives.

Earnest: If the community is the regulating mechanism—

Schulman: It's not regulating, it's *liberating*.

Earnest: —you propose the community intervene to resolve conflicts, that it is the community's "responsibility" to do that.

Schulman: I want the people around us to say that if we negotiate, in other words, if we acknowledge our participation in creating conflict, then they are still going to love us and have compassion for us. Right now if we do that it becomes a grounds for rejection.

Earnest: I am interested in this book as an argument for the direct and interpersonal as a way of working through problems together, which is increasingly rare now, even in the art world. People are very polite now, very professional, and there are few places where people have sustained serious disagreements around art or culture; when those erupt one or both parties are totally vilified.

Schulman: I don't see it as polite. I see it as entitled and increasingly assimilated into the power structures, especially the white power structure. An entire sector of white gay people, that in my time had no rights at all, are being assimilated into the white power structure and are being offered access to the punishment apparatus. It's not politeness—it's power.

Earnest: I'm in complete agreement on the level of the "personal," but when that becomes abstracted into larger entities—which your book does, moving from interpersonal to communities to religious and national groups—it breaks down. For instance, your morality is epitomized by a certain moment of gay activism, grounded in opposition to a dominant culture. The reason I asked about your Jewish background is that it is an intellectual tradition that comes out of religious belief, which then ideally creates a baseline moral and ethical imperative across the community. And so, severed from that on a larger scale, I'm not sure how we have conversations about shared moral or ethical behavior across these various, diverse "communities." I don't see where we talk about beliefs like that now.

Schulman: I don't agree with you, but I see what you're saying. I don't think it has to do with being Jewish, I think it has to do with coming from an oppression experience.

Earnest: There's a part of your interview with Andrew Sullivan from 1999 that you reproduce in *Gentrification of the Mind*, where he says, "You keep referring to extreme leftists as the community. They're not the community. They are not. They represent tiny factions of gay people in this country. We know from exit polls that 33 percent of gay people voted Republican in 1998. Imagine that is underreporting. Forty percent are voting Republican. Are they not the community? Where do they come from?" Today, Caitlyn Jenner is pro-Trump. What *does* that mean for the "gay community"?

Schulman: I think I address this directly in the book talking about white reconciliation. It's the famous Donald Suggs line that "the drag queens who started Stonewall are no better off today, but they made the world safe for gay Republicans." The more-alienated people were the ground troops that allowed those ensconced in privilege to come out. So maybe that is now entirely generational. Maybe there are entire generations of white gay people who have no oppression experience, and that is why I quote T. L. Cowen on this, that there is a "new abject object." There is a new queer. So certain white queers have been assimilated into the power structure and have access to the police. The *New Queer* is the undocumented, HIV positive, trans, poor person, person of color—they are the ones that are now the exclusive objects of the antiqueer wrath of the state because the power structure itself has not changed, it's just rearranged.

Earnest: I'm wondering how you understand the responsibility of the present generation to the past, because there is one moment in *Gentrification of the Mind* where you say, "The editors are gentrified, they don't understand their own responsibilities."

Schulman: I think it has to do with the reconciliation with the family. In my lesbian generation the leaders were Adrienne Rich and Audre Lorde. We would go to hear them speak and there would be hundreds of people in the auditorium; their books would come out and everyone would run out to read them and discuss them. That was a multigenerational community in which elders were respected. The Lesbian Herstory Archives was about reclaiming the past; "the voices we have lost" is their slogan. Because so many of us were excluded from our families we formed this multigenerational simulacral family. The queer community that I'm a part of is a community of men and women. My closest collaborator, Jim Hubbard, is a man who I worked with for thirty years; if we lived in the forties, we would have been miserably married to each other. These are all replacements by people who were excluded from biological family. But now if you're a thirty-two-year-old white lesbian and you went to Smith and you have a nice job at a publishing house and you have a nice girlfriend and you get married and your family brings you in, you don't need those other lesbians out there. You don't need those older people who made this all possible for you—you don't even have to know them or have anything to do with them because you have everything you need. So probably it's that family reconciliation and the reintegration of white gay people into the privilege machine that breaks down that relationship to the past.

Earnest: Your life unfolded at a particular time in history and you have also written histories of that period. Those are not the same thing and in some ways they seem like they might be at odds with each other. How have you navigated that?

Schulman: I say at the beginning of the book that I'm undisciplined. It's all one big thing to me—the whole thing, all one big canvas. I don't have footnotes. I never claim that anything is exactly what happened on any given day, so it is all making art to me, except that some of it is nonfiction.

Earnest: How do you see the distinction between fiction and nonfiction?

Schulman: I really don't know and I also don't know why something is nonfiction or why it is a play, I don't understand any of that.

You know I spent three months telling my shrink, *this book is crazy and when it comes out I'm going to be revealed as crazy and all the credibility I've built in thirty years is going to go down the drain.* And then I got this blurb from bell hooks and I thought, *this book is not crazy!* I just needed someone who I respected to tell me that. Everywhere I go now people are engaging me, either to disagree or discuss or grapple with it. So, amazingly, it's hit something in people, probably for two reasons that were unintended. First is the election—every time you see Trump telling you how victimized he is it's a pure enactment of what I am describing. But second is Call-Out culture, which is why I'm getting all these twenty- and thirty-year-olds at my readings because they are sick of Call-Out culture, taking each other down over nothing. Both of those things are zeitgeist.

Earnest: I want to connect this to social media as an apparatus, as a totalitarian tool, which I believe it is. Hannah Arendt describes totalitarianism as fixing and regulating people's proximity. In *The Origins of Totalitarianism* she says, "It substitutes for the boundaries and channels of communication between individual men a band of iron which holds them so tightly together that it is as though their plurality had disappeared into One Man of gigantic dimensions." What you're addressing is an effect of the way culture is structured right now through technology, in which people's relationships are held at a certain proximity, with social media seeming to offer endless connectivity and closeness while keeping people forever removed from each other. One effect is that the boundaries between public and private selves have dissolved within discourse.

Schulman: Here is an example of that: I have trolls falsely claiming that my book is, of all bizarre things, "pro-police." I ask them what they are referring to and they have nothing. So then I offer them a free copy of the book, and only two people took it. They don't want to read it, they just want to keep spamming falsities. So then I say, *can we talk on the phone?* No, they don't want to talk on the phone and they have paranoid reasons for that. They want to have a Facebook chat *so that they have a record*—for what! We're not going to court, you don't need a record! Anyway, they insist on this laborious back-and-forth in which there is no affect so nothing can be resolved, but this is mirrored in real relationships, in which people hide behind technology, or use email to make unilateral accusations that absolve their own real feeling or participation. They won't pick up the phone because then there might be some love there, some connection revealed, and the responsibility of that is unbearable. It is easier to see oneself as victimized, instead of repressed, or projecting, or anxious rooted in experiences from the past that this current person did not create.

Earnest: My experience is that when misunderstandings happen it is *impossible* to fix them via text message.

Schulman: Given that, one of the questions I ask in the book is, *why would you rather have an enemy than a conversation?* Given that people know that they can't fix it by text, why do they refuse to talk? Because they want the victimization. There is a commodity to seeing oneself as persecuted. Once you recognize that you're participating in creating a conflict you give up that commodity, which is constructed to entitle you to compassion.

Earnest: You've developed your own form of nonfiction which is personally driven but not autobiographical, historically and theoretically attuned but impressionistic. At the beginning of *Conflict Is Not Abuse* you write, "I now am able to ask you to read this book the way you would watch a play: not to emerge saying, 'The play is right!' but rather to observe that the play reveals human nuance, contradiction, limitation, joy, connection, and the tragedy of separation." How did you get to that?

Schulman: Well, I just realized that. That is the first time I figured that out. When *Empathy* (1992) first came out Kate Millet wrote this blurb that got truncated and didn't actually appear, but she said it was "the American thought-sentence." That is how she described the way it was written, and I always thought that was accurate. Because I write so much there is a lot that is just ongoing, though the genres are sometime unclear.

Earnest: However, in a way it seems like saying "I'm writing this as an artist" is a caveat positioned to wiggle out of the hard spots of making an argument.

Schulman: No. I wrote this play about Carson McCullers that was developed at the Sundance lab, and Diane Paulus, who now runs American Repertory Theater, was there as a beginner director and she looked at the play and said, *I can't figure out how you did that—you didn't take sides—* and she was referring to my depiction of the difficult marriage between Reeves and Carson McCullers, and I didn't. It's one of the reasons why my novel *The Child* (2007) about a romantic and sexual relationship between a forty-year-old man and fifteen-year-old teenager was so hard to publish, because everyone kept saying, *you don't come out against their relationship.* It's always been my view that as a novelist my job is to take it from the character's point of view. So, that way of telling a story, where I'm not taking sides in certain ways, maybe that is where my form comes from.

Earnest: Memoir or autobiographical writing is an increasingly popular mode within critical and theoretical texts. One of the complexities of writing about historical events you've experienced is that you've also lived it. I kept thinking while reading *Gentrification of the Mind* as you're chronicling the changes of the East Village during your life there, that you were also, like, twenty-three at the time; how can one disentangle the sensations and excitement of your life as a twenty-three-year-old in the East Village from your later historical analysis of what was going on at the time?

Schulman: AIDS starts when I'm twenty-three. One of the great interviews in the ACT UP oral history is with Cesar Carrasco, and he talks about how we are this phenomenon of these people who experienced a plague, and there are not a lot of examples of that in history. Time moves on and nobody else is going to experience it the way that we experienced it and we are going to die out and it affects us forever and everything we look at is going to be through that lens. I'm saying what that's like. We all read hundreds of different writers, so all this different information about experience just becomes a cumulative thing, it's not just like we're reading one person.

Earnest: What are some models you've looked toward in writing nonfiction?

Schulman: Adrienne Rich wrote this really important article "Compulsory Heterosexuality and Lesbian Existence" (1980) that was kind of like the Communist Manifesto of my generation, which can almost not be read now, because tonally it's so completely not of this moment. It reads like someone who is very enraged. It's amazing because it bursts open all these paradigms about what's "objective," what's "natural." Then Audre Lorde, who was my college professor, wrote "The Transformation of Silence into Language and Action" (1978), in which she describes being diagnosed with breast cancer and realizes that all the things that she's said in her life that got her in trouble, that even if she had never said them, she would still have breast cancer, and she comes up with this insight that *your silence will not protect you.* Those are my models of "nonfiction." They are both extremely emotional and experiential.

Earnest: Emotion is a troubled category—the whole pull of Donald Trump is emotional. The reason emotions have been figured as bad within art and discourse is that they are so unstable and easily manipulatable. But it seems to me that the "antidote" is not the suppression or banishment of emotion but to attend seriously to the emotional realities that are at play. A lot of *Conflict Is Not Abuse* is about that. How could we approach the emotional components of our discourse?

Schulman: These are my suggestions: talk in person. Ask other people to help you negotiate. And try to go through the order of events so that each person can understand what the other person's perspective is even if they can't agree with it. More communication, not less. It's not a guarantee, because what's going on now is not working.

The PEN Ten with Sarah Schulman

PEN America / 2017

From PEN.org, June 19, 2017. Reprinted with permission.

The PEN Ten is PEN America's weekly interview series. This week, we're republishing our 2016 interview with Sarah Schulman. A multifaceted writer, journalist, and AIDS historian, Schulman is cofounder of the ACT UP Oral History Project and the MIX NYC Queer Experimental Film Festival. An active member of PEN America, Schulman is Distinguished Professor of the Humanities at College of Staten Island (CUNY), a fellow at the New York Institute for the Humanities at NYU, on the Advisory Board of Jewish Voice for Peace, and faculty advisor to Students for Justice in Palestine.

Schulman will participate in PEN America's *Reading for AIDS Remembrance* this Thursday, June 22, at the AIDS Memorial in New York City.

PEN Ten: When did being a writer begin to inform your sense of identity?

Sarah Schulman: When I was six I wrote down, "When I grow up I will write books." So, I always knew. I experience this drive as a calling, something neurological.

PT: Whose work would you like to steal without attribution or consequences?

SS: My parents had the cast album of *The Threepenny Opera* because a guy from my father's hometown—Elizabeth, New Jersey—was in the chorus. I was addicted to this record. I listened over and over, and finally I got my father's typewriter and started typing out the lyrics. I was so connected to the lyrics that I needed the experience of physicalizing them.

PT: Obsessions are influences—what are yours?

SS: What actually happened. The order of events.

PEN Ten: What's the most daring thing you've ever put into words?

SS: Too many to choose from, although "A Woman's Life Is a Human Life" was up there.

PT: When, if ever, is censorship acceptable?

SS: If you mean by a government, I would say never. The real question is what drives the desire to consume another person's humiliation, and that is worth facing and understanding.

PT: What is the responsibility of the writer?

SS: Not much beyond the responsibility of anyone else.

PT: While the notion of the public intellectual has fallen out of fashion, do you believe writers have a collective purpose?

SS: Not at all.

PT: Have you ever been arrested? Care to discuss?

SS: 1979: Mob Action and Resisting Arrest. For opposing the University of Chicago giving Robert McNamara an award for "international understanding."

1982: Disruption of Congress. For interrupting a congressional anti-abortion hearing for a bill called the Human Life Statute that would have outlawed abortion and many forms of birth control. A witness was testifying that "a fetus is an astronaut in a uterine spaceship," and five other women and I jumped on our chairs and said, "A Woman's Life Is a Human Life." The arresting officer, Billy Joe Pickett, testified that I had said, "Ladies should be able to choose." I think that the idea of a woman's life being a human life was too complex.

1991: Resisting Arrest. For participating in ACT UP's Day of Desperation action at Grand Central Station to oppose the start of the First Gulf War. Our demands were: "Money for AIDS, Not for War," and "Fight AIDS, Not Arabs."

1990s: Resisting Arrest. Arrested five times with the Irish Lesbian and Gay Organization for trying to march in the Saint Patrick's Day Parade, which banned gay Irish people from marching under their own banner.

1992: Fare-beating. My girlfriend and I were very late, and the line for the token booth at Astor Place was up the staircase, so we ran through the gate and jumped on the train. We were arrested, handcuffed, marched through the East Village, and put in a cell underneath the Union Square station. When I went to court, I was sentenced to one day of community service for ACT UP.

PT: What book would you send to the leader of a government that imprisons writers?

SS: "The Transformation of Silence into Language and Action" by Audre Lorde.

PT: Where is the line between observation and surveillance?

SS: Listening, noticing, and understanding are desirable and necessary goals. A corporation wanting your Social Security number is an entirely other matter.

How to Deal with Conflicts about Ex-Lovers, HIV, Trump, and More

Trent Straube / 2018

From *POZ*, June 11, 2018. Copyright 2018 CDM Publishing, LLC. Reprinted with permission.

Want a simple way to massively improve your well-being? Then make the time to read *Conflict Is Not Abuse: Overstating Harm, Community Responsibility, and the Duty of Repair*. It's the latest book by AIDS activist and historian Sarah Schulman. As the title hints, the nonfiction work unpacks the ways we mistake conflict for abuse. Along the way, it offers methods that can be used to resolve a disagreement, whether it's a fight with an ex-lover, an ideological clash with a college lecturer, or a geopolitical quagmire (think Palestine and Israel).

"We're in a time in society where nothing is organized toward reconciliation and repair, and everything is about scapegoating and shunning," Schulman tells *POZ*. "Everyone is having this problem." Indeed we are. Which is why this book is so helpful.

During our interview, which takes place in her East Village apartment—where she has lived since 1979!—Schulman weaves in current controversies (Trump, HIV criminalization) and provocative viewpoints (white gay male oppression, the "myth" of female-to-male HIV transmission) while tracing AIDS history (ACT UP memories) and explaining new ideas (homonationalism).

Despite her intimidating résumé—distinguished professor at the City University of New York, Guggenheim and Fulbright fellowship recipient, cofounder of the Lesbian Avengers, codirector of the ACT UP Oral History Project and much more—Schulman communicates her ideas, both in the book and in this interview, in clear, accessible language. And both will leave you with much to think about.

Trent Straube: Thanks for writing this book. I wish I had read it twenty years ago—it would have saved me so much drama and self-inflicted anxiety.
Sarah Schulman: Me too.
TS: It was especially interesting to read this book in the age of Trump.
SS: He's the proof that my theories were correct! He was elected two weeks after my book came out. Every day, he tells us, "It's a witch hunt and [that] it's so sad what a victim he is." But he's the perpetrator, and then he blames Muslims and immigrants for the things actually caused by the white 1 percent, like the globalization of jobs.

But he also uses this very nationalist concept of loyalty that's part of the problem of why people get shunned by cliques and families. The problem is that loyalty is defined by joining with other people to hurt somebody. [In the book] I talk about Zionism in the Israel state, and they use this system profoundly.

TS: Reading that section, I was embarrassed I didn't know more about the issue, from the Palestinian point of view.
SS: If you read the *New York Times*, you will learn nothing about it.
TS: Your book also addresses conflicts that occur in more intimate person-to-person situations. What's your general advice for those who find themselves in an argument or conflict? Any simple steps to move forward?
SS: Real friends and healthy families encourage negotiation, and bad groups encourage escalation and shunning and blame. Our friends should help us talk to each other. When having trouble with someone, ask a friend to help you. We need to intervene in families and cliques at every level.
TS: You also recommend no texting when having a disagreement.
SS: There are people who don't take phone calls, and it's so wrong. You must talk to people.
TS: The book has an entire section related to HIV, and the title is a doozy: "HIV Criminalization in Canada: How the Richest Middle Class in the World Decided to Call the Police on HIV-Positive People in Order to Cover Up Their Racism, Guilt, and Anxiety about Sexuality and Their Supremacy-Based Investment in Punishment." Wow.
SS: Why be cruel to people? That's the larger question. So when we look at HIV criminalization, first of all, it makes no sense in any rational system. There are forty million people in the world who are HIV positive and they were all infected by someone. If we're going to say that's a crime, we're talking about incarcerating tens of millions of people.

So what purpose does it serve? When you look at empty scapegoating, in most cases it's a deflection of social anxieties. With HIV, even though there are a lot worse diseases you can have, the stigma remains and is in fact increasing—and that has nothing to do with the actual lived reality of the illness. But in the subconscious of the world, HIV is linked to queer anal sex and needle use, so there's an enormous amount of anxiety. And there's also anxiety about sex anyway, for everyone. This anxiety could be addressed in the complete opposite strategy, and that would be for governments to say, "Hey, everybody, it's time to forget about HIV stigma. Let's see what we can do to help people instead of punishing them." Instead, they're going in the direction of really brutalizing and subjugating people with HIV in a way that's [deflecting] from what's really happening socially, which is that the state is getting more and more power—because this whole incarceration system is based on sexual partners or lovers denouncing their partners to the state. A better alternative, instead of panic, is for their friends to help them deal with that anxiety.

TS: Back to the HIV chapter title. You mention the middle class's "supremacy-based investment in punishment." Can you elaborate on that aspect?

SS: It's this idea that people think they're better than others and need to reinforce that. Therefore, they subjugate others to reinforce the idea they're better. I started thinking about this when I wrote *Ties That Bind* about familial homophobia. And I realized that homophobia is not a phobia at all. [People labeled as homophobes] aren't afraid. They're enjoying it. Homophobia is a pleasure system because it makes people feel better about themselves. They need to demean others to feel better about themselves.

It's supremacy. And it's parallel to racism and any internal anxiety [like HIV fears] that we pretend is coming from outside. Instead of saying to ourselves, "Why do I feel bad when there's a Black person talking to me?" We say, "It's because he's dangerous." Actually, we're dangerous because we're having an anxiety we've been taught. But that anxiety has no basis in anything real, and instead of looking internally or getting support from other people to look internally, we're just blaming. And in this case, it's deadly.

TS: I'd like to bring up some contemporary topics playing out in the HIV community and have you assess them through the lens of conflict versus abuse.

SS: Such as "U=U"?

TS: Sure. Let's talk about the "U=U" campaign, which conveys the message that HIV is untransmittable when one's viral load is undetectable, even when condoms are not used.

SS: It's a strange argument because it's accepting the frame of completely inadequate health care. It's saying, OK, this undetectable standard for condomless sex is going to stigmatize poor people who can't access the standard of care. The problem isn't the inequality of stigma but the inequality of care.

People ask, "Is there going to be an AIDS activist movement again?" [I say] only if it lives inside a broad health care movement will it be effective. I don't understand why the arguments aren't aimed toward universal health care. Because let's face it, if everyone HIV positive had standard-of-care treatment, the need for something like PrEP [preexposure prophylaxis] would be way, way reduced. The whole existence of PrEP—a huge profit for Gilead [Sciences, the manufacturers of Truvada as PrEP]—is predicated on the lack of a [universal] health care system. If we had a health care system, they wouldn't be making money.

TS: I've seen some U=U campaigns that explicitly mention not to stigmatize those who aren't undetectable for whatever reason. And my understanding is that the U=U messaging has helped people who didn't know the science behind the message because they had a lot of self-imposed fear about transmitting the virus.

SS: It's a reform on a larger problem that needs a revolution.

TS: Have you observed areas where the HIV community has gone from being a victim to more of an abuser?

SS: Sure. Look at the "end of AIDS" claims [messaging that the epidemic is basically ending] by [HIV-positive journalist] Andrew Sullivan. Or the David France rhetoric that "we've survived a plague." And those voices, which are basically white gay men who have access to health care, have huge amounts of power in mainstream American media, and they have closed ranks around that decision. The fact that Andrew Sullivan is the person who reviewed David France's book [*How to Survive a Plague*] in the *New York Times* is a clear example of how they own the media coverage and how other realities are not getting through. This has made it so much more difficult and so damaging for the one-third of HIV-positive people who can't access standard of care.

Also even in corporate entertainment. This year, there are revivals of three significant white gay male plays: *Boys in the Band*, *Torch Song Trilogy*, and *Angels in America*. And I'm like, What is the point of reviving all this? It's a kind of white gay male oppression, when there are so many other voices that need to be heard. I don't see what it is serving, and I don't see discourse accompanying it by the people who are producing it. Because that constituency is not the constituency under attack and being oppressed now. What kind of gay men are under attack? Undocumented, people of color and poor people. And the way that people position these plays is to reinforce the brilliance of the playwrights but not to expand their concepts of which people need attention and support. Even in *Angels in America*, the message at the end is that

AZT [an early HIV med] will save us, and that wasn't even true in 1991 when the play premiered. That's the plot point: He steals the AZT. It's so irrelevant. *Angels in America* doesn't really show people fighting. ACT UP was founded in 1987 and *Angels in America* premiered in 1991, and it doesn't acknowledge that there's an activist movement out there. It really bypasses that.

TS: So are some people within the HIV community guilty of a type of supremacy ideology? If so, who would suffer from that?

SS: It's about race. I was born in 1958, but in my generation, familial homophobia was a force of history. So many gay people were driven out of their small towns or families. Even though there was always incredible racism in the gay community, we were separated from the full privilege of white supremacy because we were kicked out of our families.

But once we started to get into gay marriage and the gay nuclear family and all that, a lot of people were let back in their families. A lot of my gay friends, when they had children, their families came around. You could kind of rejoin whiteness. So now we see that white gay people who are citizens have a whole set of privileges that queer people who are undocumented or poor or of color don't have access to. And we haven't addressed that.

If you ask me what is the most pressing issue for gay people, I would say poverty.

TS: Actually, I planned to ask you what the most pressing issue for the HIV community is.

SS: It's health care. In the history of ACT UP, there was a conflict between people who had a more radical view and wanted it to be health care reform and people who were focused on drugs-in-bodies ideology. Some were radical people like Vito Russo and Marty Robinson. They died, but initially [health care reform] was their impulse.

TS: What other HIV-themed topics have your attention nowadays?

SS: I'm looking at a few things. Why are women responding more slowly to PrEP? [PrEP, or preexposure prophylaxis, refers to [the] daily pill Truvada that can prevent HIV-negative people from contracting the virus.] I think the answer is because there weren't enough studies done on women when the drugs were developed. And why are there big campaigns to get women to use PrEP, when I think PEP [postexposure prophylaxis] is something that, culturally, women will respond to more? Because there's this stigma against being prepared to have sex. So because of sexism, it seems to me, PEP would be easier to take culturally.

Then there's a large question of female-to-male HIV transmission, which has never been proved in North America. It's been an issue for a long time. I mean, way back in the eighties this was an issue. Later on, the WHO [World Health Organization] studies saw that transmission [did occur but] was connected to circumcision. At first we didn't know that, but we could see anecdotally [in North America, where most men are circumcised, that if there were common female-to-male transmission], then straight men would have HIV, and they don't. Yet even in Canada, [HIV-positive] women are incarcerated, and here it's been used primarily to oppress female sex workers when actually they are the people who are endangered. So that whole myth needs to be cleared up.

TS: It's surprising this isn't discussed more often.

SS: The reason it got suppressed as a subject is that if straight men realized that they couldn't get it from women, then they wouldn't use condoms. So in a way, the false myth saves women's lives. This was an overt discussion even in the eighties. There's a long thread in AIDS history as women being seen as vectors of infection.

TS: Another fascinating concept brought up in your book is homonationalism. I'd never heard that term. Can you describe it for our readers?

SS: The term was coined by Jasbir K. Puar, a, professor at Rutgers. This idea is that as white gay people—or Jewish gay people in the Israeli case—as they gain full rights [like marriage equality], they start to identify with the state and they start to turn on other people who are now the new scapegoats, and they become nationalists. We see movements like this in the Netherlands and even here and in England, where we see gay people turning against immigrants and Muslims and identifying with the state. Even the fight to get into the military in the United States was a fight to get into a machine that is arbitrarily killing Arabs and Muslims all over the world. So part of gaining gay rights has been about becoming part of state apparatuses that are profoundly unjust.

TS: Does homonationalism have any effect on the HIV community?

SS: "Gay" and "AIDS" got separated in the marriage equality debate. If you analyze the propaganda of the gay marriage campaigns, none of the male couples in the posters were ever identified as HIV positive. And I think the subtext on which gay marriage was sold to America was that it implied monogamy, even though we know it doesn't mean that. But they thought it did. I think they saw it as a corrective to this uncontrollable gay male sexuality. In a subtextual way, gay marriage was sold as an alternative or end to AIDS. When that happened, "AIDS" and "gay" got separated so you stopped seeing gay things that have an organic HIV content.

TS: How do you think this has affected younger LGBT people growing up in the age of gay marriage?

SS: It's horrible. There's no public space for people who are HIV positive. There are no public gatherings. It's not anything people know what to do with. Which is probably why so many people don't want to get tested.

TS: Pivoting to another topic: You have yet another book coming out, a reissue titled *My Americana History: Lesbian and Gay Life during the Reagan/Bush Years*. What's it about?

SS: It's my journalism from 1980 to 1993. And, boy, is that an interesting, wild ride. It starts with Ronald Reagan getting elected and there's no sign of HIV, and then AIDS explodes and I'm covering all this stuff. For example, I covered the closing of bathhouses for the *New York Native* [a now-defunct LGBT newspaper]. That's an interesting event because why would they send me? I was never even allowed in the bathhouses.

TS: Why did you get that assignment?

SS: Because everything was so chaotic! We didn't even know what the stories were. And also, journalists were dying. And there was no internet. For that article, I interviewed every existing organization at the time and asked them if they opposed or supported the closing. And each organization had a different point of view, and nobody knew what was right. I think we all now know that that was a mistake because bathhouses were the gathering places, and if you wanted to do AIDS education, that is the place to do it.

I also covered the first case of AIDS in the Soviet Union.

TS: What was that story assignment?

SS: It was international AIDS. We [had] no idea there was a global pandemic, so the fact that someone in the Soviet Union had it was such an oddity. And another thing I covered that was very interesting was pediatric AIDS, which was huge in that day.

And I knew [activists] Michael Callen and Robert Hilferty, who are also dead. The two of them and I went to Germany to help start ACT UP. We were brought there by Rosa von Praunheim, the film director. And we failed miserably because it was too early in their epidemic and people didn't believe it was going to happen to them. But at that time, Michael believed that dextran sulfate worked [to fight HIV]. It didn't work. It was so sad. He was taking shark cartilage at the time. He was walking around with a big bag of shark cartilage he had to take through customs. And none of it worked.

One of the great [personal challenges] in all this was that we fought to get people in trials [for HIV treatments] that didn't work, and they died. That's a very difficult thing to deal with.

But another Russian thing: Jim Hubbard and I made *United in Anger* [a 2012 documentary about the history of ACT UP] and took it all over the world. And in Russia, it was right after the antigay laws were passed. They have a separate HIV movement that's straight [heterosexual] and mostly related to heroin use and one that's gay. So there were a lot of women who were desperate to get [the HIV prevention drug] Truvada because they wanted to have children. And in Russia, all the drugs are ordered by the government and the government was not ordering Truvada. And they were like, "How can we get it?" We're like, "We don't know. Ask Gregg Gonsalves [a US activist who works in global health issues] or someone." Then we said to them, "So what do you think about these antigay laws?" And they're like, "Oh, well, they [the gay people] are going to have to leave, but Putin is a good father." And we're like, Why are we helping these people? It's so convoluted.

TS: Back to people dying in the earlier AIDS trials and losing friends to the epidemic. What has been your self-care routine throughout all this trauma?

SS: My psychology is a weird one. [I was born in] 1958, thirteen years after the end of the Holocaust, and I come from a Holocaust family. So I grew up with this whole thing like, "They stood by and let us be killed. They knew this was happening, and they did nothing." I heard this my entire life. Children weren't protected like now. So I internalized that early, that I have a responsibility for other people. But also, the AIDS movement wasn't other people—it was us.

The interesting thing about old ACT UP people is, we fought like hell with each other and all that stuff, but we're bonded in this incredible way. It's remarkable. You'll see someone on the street from ACT UP and you'll hug them. Even, like, Peter Staley. And he and I didn't get along at all, but we made up. You're bonded because you watched your friends die. We're that generation. And no one else subsequently had the same experience because of us.

TS: You changed history.

SS: We did. We did a good job.

TS: Thank you. "ACT UP, fight back, fight AIDS."

SS: Yes, there's that bond.

The Inadvertent Postmodernist: A Conversation with Sarah Schulman

Alex Dueben / 2018

From *The Rumpus*, August 29, 2018. Reprinted with permission of the author.

For more than three decades, Sarah Schulman has been one of our greatest and most vital writers. Her body of work as a novelist, nonfiction writer, playwright, and screenwriter is immense, but Schulman has also been a model as an artist who is also a passionate activist. Schulman was a member of ACT UP, a cofounder of the Lesbian Avengers, and cofounded the ACT Up Oral History Project.

In novels like *The Cosmopolitans*, *People in Trouble*, *Shimmer*, and *The Child*, Schulman has documented the postwar era, tackling questions of politics, sexuality, gender, race, and abuse through individual experience. Her nonfiction books, including *Stagestruck*, *Ties That Bind*, and *The Gentrification of the Mind*, tackle a wide variety of issues, one of the reasons Schulman was once called "the lesbian Susan Sontag." More than delivering the final word on subjects like the meaning of gentrification, and the true costs of familial homophobia, she wants to open a discussion about the implications of those ideas.

In September, Schulman's mystery novel *Maggie Terry* is being released by The Feminist Press. The titular character is a former NYPD detective whose first day out of rehab in her new job as a private detective involves investigating the murder of a young actress. In between AA and NA meetings, Terry tries to confront her past, including her dead partner, her vindictive ex, and the daughter she's desperate to see again, even as she struggles to find stability in a changing city and an unsteady nation. Also this fall her nonfiction work *My American History: Lesbian and Gay Life during the Reagan/Bush Years*, is being reissued in a twenty-fifth anniversary edition.

Recently, Schulman and I discussed how *Maggie Terry* connects with the themes of her other books, the mystery genre, and why she can't ever write a novel that's didactic.

The Rumpus: In the author's note for *Maggie Terry*, you mention the murder of Eric Garner. Was that an impetus for the book?

Sarah Schulman: Not really. I wrote it in layers. I had a lot of different versions and each time I worked on it, I added another subplot or theme. The final layers were last summer. I have been teaching in Staten Island for twenty years, and in my classes there about 15 percent of my students are police officers, correctional officers, Port Authority police, and their families and children. They've been consistently a presence in my class. When Eric Garner was killed I said to the class, we have to stop and deal with this. What was remarkable was that I had white, Latino, and Black kids who were from cop families in that class, and they all supported the police. Not one of them criticized the role of the police. They were saying, *If Eric Garner had just done what he was told, he'd be alive today.* That was one of the first times I really put it all on the table with the students. I find that the ones who come from police families, they're very embedded in their families and it's very hard for them to question the police. They feel like they're being disloyal.

Rumpus: You said that you wrote *Maggie Terry* in stages and layers. What was the initial stage?

Schulman: In the first stage, Maggie was straight. Originally this was [a] TV pilot that I wrote, and then I decided to novelize it. I tend to have lots of layers in my books. Often in my first draft I'll just write the story and then I start to develop the subplots. What are the other nuances that are converging on the theme? I don't think that anything is simple, so I'm never looking for simple answers. I'm trying to look at multiplicities of experience.

Rumpus: You closed the introduction to *The Gentrification of the Mind* by writing, "This book is my effort to find awareness about what was lost, what replaced it, and how to move forward to a more authentic and conscious and just way to live." I kept thinking that's what Maggie is trying to do in the new novel.

Schulman: I'm only just realizing this, that from the beginning—my first book came out in 1984—that all of my books are actually *Conflict Is Not Abuse*. There have been certain fundamental beliefs that I've held from the beginning. Only recently have I become aware of what they were. I think Maggie is very much part of that. My job as a novelist is to reveal how people understand their own lives. Not how we wish they would understand, but how they actually understand them. I have characters believing things and doing things that perhaps the reader would not want them to, but that's what people do. That's what I'm most interested in, capturing the complexity but also, more importantly, the vulnerability that is behind being human.

Rumpus: You are very prolific and I kept thinking about *Maggie Terry* in relation to your early novel *After Delores*, which is sort of a mystery about addiction and traumatizing relationships and AA and the changing city.

Schulman: My first book, *The Sophie Horowitz Story*, has some similar themes. The one thing they all have in common is that they're funny. I have this strange idea of genre. I write historical fiction or experimental fiction or literary fiction or speculative fiction or detective fiction, but it's never really locked within the genre boundaries. I think I was an inadvertent postmodernist from the beginning because I just never adhered to formula very well.

Rumpus: It plays with the genre but it works as a mystery.

Schulman: It's got this noirish feel. I read Dashiell Hammett last summer and it was so fantastic. Maybe that was in my mind when I was writing the final draft. Hammett has gay people and Black people; he has everybody. It's quite interesting. His range of characters is remarkable. I was really surprised, but he was a lefty and had this inclusive worldview.

Rumpus: *The Sophie Horowitz Story* and *After Delores* were crime books, and you were writing at a time when there weren't many openly lesbian crime writers writing about lesbian characters.

Schulman: *Sophie Horowitz* was the third lesbian detective novel and I wasn't aware of any of the others.

Rumpus: People like Ellen Hart and Mary Wings came a few years after. Were you conscious of turning away from writing that kind of book?

Schulman: No. I just write whatever I want. My second book, *Girls, Visions and Everything*, was experimental. I just write whatever I want. I'm not calculating in that way.

Rumpus: You've always seemed interested in writing a different book each time.

Schulman: It comes out differently. The whole thing is very hard to explain. Why something is a mystery. Why one thing is a play and another thing is a book. Why is this historical fiction, and why is this literary fiction? I don't know the answers to these questions. They're impulse issues.

Rumpus: I was looking at [a] timeline of your books and in the past decade you've written a lot of nonfiction, or you've published a lot of nonfiction.

Schulman: There were ten years when I couldn't publish anything, so a lot of that was written during that time and suddenly it was all published together. Sometimes it takes forever for someone to be like, *Oh, that's a good idea.*

Rumpus: Books like *The Gentrification of the Mind* and *Ties That Bind* are about issues you'd been thinking about for years.

Schulman: *Stagestruck* was decades ahead in recognizing that the gay movement was being turned into a niche market. *Israel/Palestine* was really on the brink of a transformation of consciousness for the queer community about the Israeli occupation. It's interesting because when *After Delores* came out it was really the first modern lesbian novel to get a review in the *New York Times*. People were so excited; they thought everything was going to change. Here we are thirty years later and none of these books have been made into movies. Because they're so much about looking at it from a certain point of view. That kind of view has never been allowed to be represented in a large way. I'm still waiting for people to catch up. I'm going to turn sixty in two weeks. I've been waiting a long time. [*Laughs*]

Rumpus: I read *Shimmer* years ago and in the opening scene—I can hear you laughing because you know what I'm about to read—"How could a person have written so many books and still not be able to earn a living. Still be so unknown." When I read it years ago I was like, that's not how it works, and now that I'm over thirty, that's pretty much every writer I know.

Schulman: I have two favorite things that have ever been said about me. One was when *Publishers Weekly* said I was one of the most underrated writers in America. Being constantly underrated is a very interesting experience—especially contrasted to people who are overrated. What a writer wants more than money or power is to know that they're a good writer. People who are overpraised know they're overpraised. That's a problem I've never had. The other is that the *Los Angeles Times* once called me the lesbian Susan Sontag. I just love that because it says it all about the transactional reputation to be found and the deals you make with the devil.

On the other hand, my communities have been incredibly supportive of me. I get an email or a Facebook message or a Twitter note every single day from somebody telling me that some book was important to them. This has been going on for years. Readers don't ever let me feel abandoned. It's the system. The difference between the system and the readers has just gotten more and more pronounced. I could not get *Conflict Is Not Abuse* published in the United States. I had to publish it in Canada. I thought, no one is going to read this book. It didn't get any prepublication reviews, but then people started reading it and writing about it online. It went into another printing. Four months after publication, *Publishers Weekly* finally reviewed it—because people were reading it. That was just incredible. My joke is that I can always tell who's queer or straight, because the queer people say, *Sarah, you've been doing so much*, and the straight people say, *So, Sarah what do you do?* That happens all the time. It's like hiding in plain sight. Often this happens with people who are incredibly successful. We all started in the same place, and they're enormously successful and I'm just sitting here.

Rumpus: A twenty-fifth anniversary edition of *My American History* comes out this fall, and I think this is one of the books to understand the 1980s and where we are today. What's in this new edition?

Schulman: Urvashi Vaid wrote the initial introduction twenty-five years ago and she wrote the updated introduction for the new edition. We also found some old stuff that Alison Bechdel and I had done together in the eighties that we had both forgotten about. A professor unearthed them. So we're reproducing that. Steven Thrasher, a Black gay journalist with whom I'm very simpatico, did a kind of updating interview. Otherwise it's just the original material. It's incredible material that you can't find anywhere else. It starts before AIDS. It's 1980 and I'm covering Reagan and the rise of the new right and the coalition between the religious right and the Republican party. All the things that we're dealing with now, I'm covering it as it's happening. I'm covering the bathhouse closings, and AIDS arrests, and women being excluded from drug trials, and children with HIV, and homeless people, and AIDS in the Soviet Union. At the same time I'm covering lesbian culture and stories about Black women being excluded from bars. This group called Dykes Against Racism picketing those bars. I covered one of the last bar raids in New York when a Black bar called Blues was raided. It was two blocks away from the *New York Times* and it was part of the gentrifying of Times Square. All of these really key cultural moments for which there's no documentation anywhere else, all in one place. The book ends in 1994, two years before protease inhibitors, so it's the height of AIDS. Rereading it was really something. A rollercoaster that we all lived.

Rumpus: *The Gentrification of the Mind* is a sequel, in a sense, to a lot of that.

Schulman: That book is just catching on now. I had written it in that decade when I couldn't get anything published. It took years to get it published and so when it came out it was already old for me, but it's catching on now. I have a French edition coming out in September. People are calling about it and using it in their classes. I think Picasso said the imitator makes it ugly and the derivator makes it beautiful. They always tell you it's better to be the fifth person to have an idea than the first person. Of course I could not foresee what gentrification would become.

Rumpus: In one sense it was hard to reread *My American History* but in another sense I enjoyed it and felt energized by it.

Schulman: It's the foundation that created the moment we're in now that we need to be aware of. One of the things that I document in *My American History* is that the Republican Party made a coalition with the religious right around the Reagan election in 1980. What we see from history is that that's what became the Tea Party. This is what produced the Trey Gowdys and Mike Pences of the world. That wing got control of the whole party. The greedy capitalist Republicans thought they could control those people—but they couldn't. I also wrote about Trump in 1990 in *People in Trouble*. People in New York have always hated Trump. That family has been known by New Yorkers for decades. In *People in Trouble* it's interesting because what I have him doing is gentrification. Although it's not called that.

Rumpus: *People in Trouble* was the first book of yours I read and what I loved about that book (and *Rat Bohemia* and others)—and what made them stand out—was that they were about activism and activists, but they were never didactic. They were great novels and they were very political.

Schulman: Getting back to where we started, I'm very interested in all the layers. That's why these books can never be didactic. Because all of my characters are what I call vulnerable. Because they're real people. I want to understand them. That's why the *People in Trouble* transition to *Rent* is so fascinating, because [Jonathan Larson] simplifies them. He made them binary. My whole game is to understand them. And I also want to be understood. That's why I think communication is so important.

Rumpus: You've always written complicated characters and avoid simplifying them or simplifying their conflicts and differences.

Schulman: People are conflicted and confused and have pain and unfortunately project that pain—which is now completely dominating our nation. It's certainly true in the subculture. I wrote about stigmatized people from the beginning. My first book, which came out when I was twenty-four, had the first Asian lesbian character in any piece of American fiction. I struggled for a number of books with writing Black protagonists. I don't think I really succeeded until *The Cosmopolitans*. I've been trying to write the world in a way that if people who are that person read it, they would say that it was plausibly accurate. That's what I've been doing from the start because I come from that generation that was not represented. Lesbians are still not represented accurately. I see lesbian misrepresentation everywhere I go. I'm very aware of that experience. In the early days in the eighties there was this thing called the tyranny of positive images where people would create these perfect characters as a counter to the pathology, and I always hated that. I don't think that helped us. The idea was to show that you're a full person, not just an oppositional caricature. That's been part of my impulse from the start.

Rumpus: I suppose that it must be really frustrating to be ignored, to be misread, because you are trying to communicate and want to be understood. And other people and places are clearly not looking for that.

Schulman: They're looking for books that reinforce a certain value system. There's a confusion between familiarity and quality. If it tells the people in power what they already think about themselves and reflects that, then they think it's good. On the other hand, if it tells them that actually they're quite subjective and they're not neutral and might want to rethink themselves, then it's bad.

Rumpus: Art that makes them uncomfortable or is disturbing is considered "bad."

Schulman: It's the difference between art and entertainment. Entertainment tells us what we already know; art expands what we think we know. The second is more uncomfortable. You come home from work and you're exhausted and watch *Law & Order* because you know exactly what's going to happen. It's so predictable that it's relaxing. That's what a lot of books that we're told are great literature in America actually do. They're repetitive and they reflect an image that gatekeepers want of themselves. You can see it in the theater as well.

I don't know how those people live with themselves, to be honest. Sometimes I'll go see a mainstream writer give a reading and the place will be packed but the readers are not invested. Whereas in a subculture if you go see a writer, the readers care so much. It's a completely different dynamic between the writer and the reader. Why would you want to write something that doesn't matter?

Taking Responsibility: An Interview with Sarah Schulman

Carley Moore / 2018

Originally published in the *Los Angeles Review of Books* (www.lareviewofbooks.org), October 14, 2018. Reprinted with permission.

Sarah Schulman is an East Village icon and a hero to many readers and writers because she has made queer characters the protagonists in her novels, and LGBTQIA history the focus of her historical work. I was excited to talk with her about her new novel, *Maggie Terry*, because it shares some themes—gentrifying New York, queer outsiders, and parenting, to name a few—with my debut novel, *The Not Wives*. (Full disclosure: *Maggie Terry* is published by the Feminist Press, which is also publishing my book, due out next year.) The book is a page-turner and follows Maggie, an addict, an alcoholic, a former police officer who has lost custody of her daughter, as she moves through her first five days back on the job as a private investigator.

On a sunny day in late August, I walked east to Sarah's apartment. Like many New Yorkers, I noticed new stores, old stores, and empty storefronts. Astor Place is largely unrecognizable. There's a CVS, a Shake Shack, and the lipstick building (as my daughter and I call it) full of luxury condos. St. Marks still has a weird assortment of stalls and tiny stores and there are a lot of thriving boutiques and restaurants throughout the village, but banks and bros abound, and sometimes, well, it's withering. Like many of us who have managed to cling to a gentrifying New York, Maggie Terry is stunned by the changes to her city.

Sarah gave me a glass of water while we both worried over my recording app, and then we talked about *Maggie Terry*, which proved an opening for a wide-ranging discussion on everything from the dialectic between blame and responsibility, the complexity of motherhood, new opportunities for queer fiction writers, and the struggles of gentrification.

Carley Moore: *Maggie Terry* is the first murder and intrigue novel you've written in thirty years. What was it like for you to return to such a plot-driven form? What are the charms and frustrations of the mystery novel?

Sarah Schulman: It was very easy. The two books I had written before that had so much gravitas. *The Cosmopolitans* (Feminist Press, 2016) is a book I'm really proud of. I felt like it was an accomplishment, that it was a really literary book, and *Conflict Is Not Abuse: Overstating Harm, Community Responsibility, and the Duty of Repair* (Arsenal Pulp Press, 2016) was like the hardest thing I ever wrote. I just thought, I can't do this to myself again, right away.

CM: Maggie's trying to piece together a self of some kind between being an addict, an alcoholic, a former police officer, a mother who has lost custody of her daughter, and someone just getting back on their feet. She's a fuck-up who wants to get better, navigating life in a gentrified Chelsea amid the borderline apocalypse that is the Trump presidency. How does a character like Maggie speak to this particular political moment?

SS: Well, there's a couple of questions there. A really long time ago, I stopped writing protagonists that were based on myself, and I started writing protagonists based on people who were driving me crazy.

So there's a couple of people that I'm trying to figure out, and I'm sure you noticed that the book is dedicated to Thelma Wood, who was, historically, one of the world's worst girlfriends who ever lived. She was the bad girlfriend of Djuna Barnes and she drove Djuna Barnes so crazy that she was the muse for Djuna Barnes's work. So the book is dedicated to bad girlfriends.

But one of the elements in the protagonist that I'm currently plagued by is somebody whose life is a combination of alcohol and antidepressants, and when you see her, she looks like she's been drinking pain for twenty years. She looks terrible, and yet she thinks that people like me are her problem. I'm very interested in that. The question of blame. I've always been interested in the question of blame. So Maggie Terry is a person who has the disease of addiction, and is grappling with who to blame for it and, because this person in my life is doing that, I wanted to understand that.

CM: Though Trump is not the center of the book, he's definitely informing it, and stressing every character out. He's such a narcissist and in so much pain. He blames everyone for his problems, so we are grappling with that as a country, too.

SS: Yeah, it's like when I wrote my novel *Shimmer*, which is set during McCarthyism, and you're in this period where the government is so corrupt, and they're punishing people, and scapegoating people, for no legitimate reason. And you're asking people to make moral decisions about how they treat their friends in that context, and it's impossible, because there's a trickle-down of corruption. Our period now, that *Maggie Terry* is set in, when we have a president who's insane, and everyone is living in fear, has to affect how we make decisions about responsibility and accountability. And so that's one of the frames of the book. Another one is that I've been teaching on Staten Island for twenty years, and I have had a lot of police officers and their families as my students: New York Police Department, correctional officers at Rikers [Island], Port Authority Police [Department]. And listening to them justify the behavior of the police, I have so much information about how they look at it, and I really wanted to address that in the book as well. Because it's another frame of lying. There's the alcoholic who's lying, there's the police officer who's lying, and then there's the president who's lying. And yet there are those of us who are trying to figure out what's true, in the middle of all this.

CM: Maggie's former partner, Julio, had a son who is also a cop, and he shoots an African American man in a stairwell. There's a public outcry for justice, and a scandal that haunts Maggie throughout the novel. You treat the corrupt officers with empathy, while not letting them off the hook. Why do you think this approach is important in a moment when we see such urgent protests of police brutality from individuals and organizations like Black Lives Matter?

SS: Well, because it doesn't water down what's right and wrong to understand that people are fully human. In fact, it reinforces it. When I wrote *Conflict Is Not Abuse*, I suddenly realized that actually, I'd been writing *Conflict Is Not Abuse* my entire life. Every book of mine is about how there are no demons. It doesn't mean there's no right and wrong—there is. But people do things for reasons, and we need to understand what those reasons are. It's not an excuse. But to pretend that people are one-dimensional is tragic, not just socially, but intimately. There are people walking around blaming someone that they used to love, which is one of the themes of the book, for absolutely nothing. One of Maggie's concerns is that because she's the addict who screwed up, she's the one who's wrong. And then everyone in her life gets to create her as the wrong person, and they never have to look at their own participation.

CM: She's especially frustrated with Frances, her ex, and Frances's role in the end of their relationship and in Maggie's drug use.

SS: Yeah, because Frances did drugs, too, but that never comes up. Not only do we take advantage of other people—we create other people as receptacles of blame so that we don't have to look at ourselves. But also, when people have some kind of success, like Frances is in a successful relationship, so she thinks that means she's right. Like people think if their career is going well, they're right. But it's not true. Sometimes the glue of relationships is in creating a wrong together, a lie that people tell each other, and it bonds them. They can never confront it, because their relationship would shatter. Other times, it's creating a person that you know as the receptacle of evil, which is the easiest way to never, ever question yourself.

CM: That reminds me of a favorite moment in the book, Maggie's realization that "[s]ome people don't believe in the unconscious."

SS: Well, that was something that I learned with publishing *Conflict Is Not Abuse*. Because there were some people who had principled disagreements with that book, and it's the kind of book where it's impossible to agree with everything in it because there are too many ideas. So any regular, normal reader would have things they disagree with. But there were people who destroyed it, and never read it, clearly. They had probably read half the title. And I realized that their objections were not to what was in the book, but [were] to the larger issues of the unconscious. That there were people who strongly objected to the idea that they may have motivations that they're not in touch with.

CM: My students struggle with this around ideology—a larger, cultural way of thinking about the unconscious—specifically with the fact that there are ideological forces that determine how we behave. *Maggie Terry* does a lot of work around the ideology of the police state and how relationships function within it.

SS: The topic of the book is blame, on all levels, right? So you have Trump, who's blaming everybody for his flaws, and blaming people for problems that don't actually exist. And then you have Maggie as the person everybody blames because she got caught. Then you have Jamie Robbins, who can't face what her father has done to her, so she blames her lover who wants to protect her, and this blame destroys him.

False accusation, something that I've addressed in *Conflict Is Not Abuse*, is the thing that people hide behind. Whenever Trump blames things on immigrants that are actually caused by the white 1 percent, for example, he's employing false accusation. So when Jamie Robbins falsely accuses her boyfriend, Steven Brinkley, of a crime that was actually committed by her father, he can't live with that.

CM: There are also a lot of different families in the book—Maggie's broken family, her ex-wife and her daughter; the work family that she creates at her new job, and the work family that ended with the death of her partner Julio; and, of course, Maggie's AA meetings, which have this kind of loose, familial structure that keeps her afloat. Can you talk about how queer families or queer people configure families in this book?

SS: I don't view those communities as families. For me, "family" is the dirty word, so I think I once said that the two words that give me the most fear are the words "chosen family." I think it's about friends. Maggie's life has been completely destroyed, and so she has two communities. She has these meetings, she goes to NA and she goes to AA, and she never really commits to them in a certain way, but she grapples with them, and she meets people inside them. But it does help her solve a crime. The sheer humanity of people being able to admit their flaws in a world in which no one will admit their flaws is illuminating to her, and it helps in trying to understand who killed Jamie Robbins.

CM: I love the AA and the NA meetings, the 12 Steps, and the way you embed them into narrative. Those stories are so diverse and such an interesting part of the book and they become moments when people really have no one else to blame.

SS: Well also, they're allowed to take responsibility in the meetings—whereas in the real world, no one is allowed to take responsibility. Jamie Robbins couldn't take responsibility, and Frances couldn't take responsibility, and Maggie's father couldn't take responsibility.

CM: Maggie's a failed mother. I'm a mom, and I appreciate the space that you made for complicated mothers, because there's not much room for them in mainstream media. What do we come to understand about mothering in your book?

SS: Well, people use their children as weapons, right? So people who don't want to take responsibility for their role in conflict can withhold their child from an adult who actually should have access to that child. In my book on homophobia and the family, *Ties That Bind: Familial Homophobia and Its Consequences* (2009), I talk about a period when there was no legal recognition for gay relationships, and women would have a child with somebody, and then they would break up, and their punishment was to take the child away from the former partner. People say, "Oh, my sister can't see my child, because I am clean and perfect, and my sister is the embodiment of all evil." Or, "My ex cannot see the child who loves her and whom she loves, because to do that would mean having to allow contradictions, and things about myself and my own flaws into our world that I don't want to have there." These are all ways of creating a false image of perfection. It's another form of shunning, and it's extremely detrimental.

In *Maggie Terry*, it's all about whether or not Frances can accept herself as someone who also has work to do. And as long as she won't accept that, she's just going to use the child to punish Maggie.

CM: Maggie's time in rehab makes her into a kind of Rip Van Winkle for the city. She returns to Chelsea, to New York, and so much has changed. There's been so much writing about how New York has changed, including Jeremiah Moss's *Vanishing New York*, and Kevin Baker's recent essay "The Death of a Once Great City" in *Harper's Magazine*. I'm writing about this in my novel, as well; so many people are. You've also written about this in *Gentrification of the Mind: Witness to a Lost Imagination*. All these projects feel elegiac. Can we go back in time? Can we stop the malling of New York City?

SS: Well, it's a question of political will. I mean, gentrification could be ended tomorrow if we built five hundred thousand affordable housing units in New York City. If we had commercial rent control. If we fined people who buy to flip rather than buy to live. If we limited how many franchises a business can have to three, for example. If we wanted to have a livable and habitable city that produced cultural ideas for the world, we could.

CM: What are you working on now?

SS: I'm working on a lot of things. I'm doing a collaboration with Marianne Faithfull. We're doing a stage play that uses music from her fifty-year career. I have two plays in development right now. One is about the *Roe v. Wade* case; that is having a reading at New York Theatre Workshop. I'm writing a book about the history of ACT UP and that's like this massive [undertaking]. That's because Jim Hubbard and I did the ACT UP Oral History Project, which if people want to check out, is at www.actuporalhistory.org. I interviewed 187 surviving members of ACT UP over eighteen years. So I'm now cohering some of that into a book.

CM: Do you think publishing is changing for queer writers?

SS: Well, yeah. Emily Hashimoto, who was my student at Queer|Art|Mentorship, just wrote a beautiful novel about two young women of color in love, and it's going to be published commercially. Just a very short time ago, that would have been relegated to the margins of the margins.

CM: I'm thinking about Andrea Lawlor's *Paul Takes the Form of a Mortal Girl*, which started out at Rescue Press and will be reissued by a Big Six publisher.

SS: But I hope that people don't forget those of us who were here first, and all our old books. My late friend Donald Suggs once said, "The people who make change are not the people who benefit from it." And they make the world better for others. And I hope that that's not going to be what's on my tombstone, but right now, it's kind of looking like that. But we'll see.

CM: I don't want that to be on your tombstone.

SS: [*Laughs*] Okay.

What ACT UP Can Teach Us about the Current Health Emergency: An Interview with Sarah Schulman

Elisa R. Linn / 2020

From *Frieze*, June 5, 2020. Reproduced courtesy of Frieze Publishing.

On October 11, 1988, a mass of people stood outside the US Food and Drug Administration (FDA) headquarters in Rockville, Maryland. The group, which had gathered to protest the agency's slow approval process for new HIV/AIDS treatments, exhorted: "Drug into bodies!" At the time, the recycled cancer-fighting drug AZT—which had serious side effects and was egregiously expensive—was the only FDA-approved treatment available in the US. One of the AIDS Coalition to Unleash Power's (ACT UP) most successful and media-effective actions in the fight against the epidemic, the protest resulted in a breakthrough: that same week, the FDA announced new procedures to shorten the approval of life-prolonging medications by two years.

ACT UP was an activist group formed in 1987 out of anger over the inaction of politicians and the medical establishment to address the AIDS crisis. Today, as another virus sweeps across the world, ACT UP's history teaches us that the political dimension of healthcare is always bound up with questions of stigmatization, recognition and access.

According to Sarah Schulman—a longstanding member of ACT UP and the author of books such as *Conflict Is Not Abuse* (2016)—what remains crucial is resisting the portrayal of the fight against AIDS as a "progressive narrative." I spoke to Schulman about her forthcoming book, *Let the Record Show: A Political History of ACT UP, New York, 1987–1993*, which documents the movement's achievements, strategies and failures, and how far these can be helpful lessons for our current state of normalized exception.

Elisa R. Linn: How does your forthcoming book relate to the 1987 exhibition *Let the Record Show . . .*, at the New Museum in New York, which included an installation of ACT UP's iconic "Silence=Death" logo?

Sarah Schulman: In the New Museum show, ACT UP combined photographs from the Nuremberg trials, in which the Allies prosecuted Nazi war criminals after World War II, with portraits of right-wing American politicians and Cardinal Ratzinger—later Pope Benedict XVI—who sabotaged the fight against AIDS with anticondom messaging and, in a 1986 letter to Catholic bishops, defined homosexuality as "an intrinsic moral evil." ACT UP and the show's curator, William Olander, hoped that such figures would be held accountable for their actions, hence the title.

ERL: In his article "Against Agamben: Is a Democratic Biopolitics Possible?," published in *Critical Legal Thinking* in March, the journalist Panagiotis Sotiris referenced ACT UP's tactics. He writes about a possible strategy for the current COVID-19 crisis in terms of "a biopolitics from below": a form of collective self-organization that employs methods of criticism, research, intervention, destigmatization and solidarity. To what extent do you think this is possible?

SS: We are in a new era of repression and profound confusion. Medically, we are much further ahead than we were back then with AIDS. Nevertheless, the government in the US is using the same strategy: it recycles earlier drugs that pharmaceutical companies have patents for, because that is more profitable than investing in new or nascent medications. Even if a cure for COVID-19 were found tomorrow, we don't have a healthcare system that would allow people to access it. In a joint statement issued on February 27, for example, US House Speaker Nancy Pelosi and Senate Democratic Leader Chuck Schumer said that vaccines should be "affordable and available to all." They didn't say: "We need a free vaccine."

Looking at the history of progressive social movements in the US, there is usually a *zeitgeist* moment when things suddenly leap forward. Unfortunately, you can never force it. Current movements can learn the following from ACT UP: coalition, simultaneity and direct action. That combination is crucial to enable any movement to succeed. If your demands are too vague and too large, you can't win. Also, it is necessary to understand what a campaign is. Don't waste your energy on poorly planned actions: ensure everything is carefully orchestrated to have maximum impact.

ERL: You coproduced the documentary film *United in Anger* (2012) and initiated the ACT UP Oral History Project (2001–ongoing) with ACT UP activist and filmmaker Jim Hubbard. These look at the movement from the perspective of people fighting the epidemic. Is your new book aiming to use this material?

SS: ACT UP was an organizational nexus that reached into the broader AIDS coalition: prison inmates, mothers, drug users, homeless people, migrants, activists. I wrote to people and asked them: "What do you have in your private collection?" One of my favorite photographs that I received in response was taken during a 1991 trial against eight ACT UP members who had been providing clean hypodermic needles to drug addicts to prevent them from contracting AIDS. It shows a lesbian lawyer arguing in court for three of her defendants: one is a trans woman (Kathy Otter), one is a gay Black man (Dan Keith Williams) and one is a straight white woman (Debra Levine). This could have been the emblematic photo of ACT UP, but it wasn't what the media wanted at the time. It's time to change how we visualize resistance.

ACT UP never theorized itself. There was no big picture initially, although over the years we accrued one. One of the essential points I want to address in my new book is what a broad coalition it was. A very false image of ACT UP has evolved over the last few years. Images ingrained in the collective memory are of a white male protestor, in a white T-shirt and black leather jacket, being dragged away by police.

ERL: This shows how representation can flatten complexity and is capable of functioning repressively.

SS: Yes, real people cannot be summed up—and that's true for the movements they create, as well.

ERL: Do you see your new book as a way to conceive something like a "people's history'"?

SS: My focus is on helping other people organizing today because, as I see it, ACT UP was the most successful recent activist social movement in the US. I'm providing a summary of what our strategies were, how they were implemented and whether they worked or not. Interestingly, ACT UP did not use a consensus model. It allowed everyone to respond personally. So, for example, if you wanted to disrupt mass at St Patrick's Cathedral—as some members did in 1989—and I didn't want to, I wouldn't prevent you from doing it; I just wouldn't participate. There was no attempt to control or stop each other, and allowing many responses to take place simultaneously proved to be a winning strategy.

ACT UP operated in exceptional circumstances, since its members were continually dying, so leadership emerged and changed naturally. We had a big meeting every Monday, with maybe five hundred to eight hundred people attending. There was a coordinating committee with representatives from each smaller committee. There were also affinity groups, consisting of ten or twenty people who weren't accountable to the larger group. The only thing that everyone had to agree on was one key principle: "direct action to end the AIDS crisis." What form that action could take was defined very broadly.

ERL: How were issues such as privilege discussed inside the movement?

SS: There were a lot of discussions around issues of citizenship and immigration status. However, when people are dying, privilege is a much more complicated issue. There were no treatments early on. For a person who was very sick to get arrested during an ACT UP protest and put in a cell was a huge sacrifice. Once treatments became available, the inequality became even greater, since we don't have a functional healthcare system in the US.

ERL: Speaking about the AIDS pandemic in your film *United in Anger*, Zoe Leonard described it as "a crisis of society"? Do you think the same can be said of COVID-19?

SS: Right now, BAME and PoC are dying in the US in very high numbers. I'm in Chicago, where 30 percent of the population is Black but accounts for 70 percent of deaths from COVID-19. When there is a cataclysm in the US, it reveals the fissures in society: things that were already in crisis—profound inequalities, profound biases—become starkly highlighted. During the AIDS crisis, it was mostly marginalized people without rights who were affected, so in that regard the current situation is quite similar. However, unlike the present moment, the wider public didn't know or care about the AIDS crisis at all. It wasn't on television. There was no national plan and no collective concern. It was a private disaster. In that sense, it was quite different.

Good Conflict

Molly Fischer / 2020

From *The Cut*, August 2, 2020, https://www.thecut.com/2020/08/sarah-schulman-conflict-is-not-abuse.html. Reprinted with permission of VOX Media, LLC.

Sarah Schulman is a playwright, an author, and a queer activist. She is also a professor of creative writing, and once, a number of years ago, she learned that a male graduate student maintained a blog where he wrote about his crush on her. He wrote that he was in love with her; he wrote that he wanted to fuck her; he wrote about her appearance in a way that made her feel bad. She told her colleagues what was happening, and their response was unanimous: He was "stalking" her. They advised Schulman to report him to a supervisor.

She considered this. She was uncomfortable with what was happening, and she wanted it to stop. But she was also uncomfortable with her colleagues' advice. "I realized that the more I saw myself as being victimized by this person, the more support I had from my colleagues," Schulman told me. "They would wrap me in the comfort of their protection. And I found this very disturbing. Because no one said to me, 'Why don't you ask him what he thinks is going on?'"

In her mind, *stalking* meant something like "when your ex-husband is in front of your house with a gun." She wasn't frightened of her student; she was disconcerted. "Stalking is a real thing, and people lose their lives to stalking," Schulman said. What she had on her hands was not that: It was a situation in which "somebody is feeling something and another person feels uncomfortable about it. That is often called stalking, but it's not stalking." She decided to call her student and talk to him about it.

She learned, first of all, what a blog was and what sorts of things people wrote there—this was the early aughts, and she hadn't really known. So there was a generational divide at work. She also learned she was the first teacher who had taken his writing seriously; he'd probably gotten "overinvolved" because of that. They had a few conversations, he said what he wanted to say, she transferred him to another adviser, and no further issues arose. Looking back, "the scary thing was how much reward was waiting for me if I presented myself as victimized," she said—that promise of community embrace.

Schulman describes this episode in a book she wrote some years later, *Conflict Is Not Abuse*. The book's central insight is that people experiencing the inevitable discomfort of human misunderstanding often overstate the harm that has been done to them—they describe themselves as victims rather than as participants in a shared situation. And overstating harm itself can cause harm, whether it leads to social shunning or physical violence.

Schulman argues that people rush to see themselves as victims for a variety of reasons: because they're accustomed to being unopposed, because they're accustomed to being oppressed, because it's a quick escape from discomfort—from criticism, disagreement, confusion, and conflict. But when we avoid those uncomfortable feelings, we avoid the possibility of change. Instead, Schulman wants friends to hold each other accountable, ask questions, and intervene to help each other talk through disagreements—not treat "loyalty" as an excuse to bear grudges.

A wide-ranging exploration of human relationships and responsibility, *Conflict Is Not Abuse* was the rare book published in October 2016 to be more relevant instead of less by November's end. It was a book for which Schulman could find no US publisher; which was released by Arsenal Pulp, a queer Canadian press that paid her a $2,500 advance; and which—like *Debt*, by David Graeber, or *All about Love*, by bell hooks—was the kind of accessible work that wins a radical figure unexpected fans. The book offers readers a clarifying lens through which to consider the fraught encounters of our era of discontent: between police and protesters; between writers and their readers; between colleagues, neighbors, and friends. It is now in its seventh printing.

Clear, provocative and concise, "conflict is not abuse" is a perfectly aerodynamic unit of intellectual achievement. It has flown farther, faster, than Schulman ever thought it would. In part, this is because the mantle of victimhood she argues against has become more widely recognized and discussed even as it has remained exceedingly commonplace. Claudia Rankine, a friend of Schulman's for nearly thirty years, said the Central Park encounter between Amy Cooper and Christian Cooper was emblematic of the pattern Schulman describes. Christian Cooper was birding in May when he asked Amy Cooper to follow park rules and leash her dog; she responded by calling the police and claiming she was in danger. "It's a threat that is imagined but then weaponized in a society that is systemically racist," Rankine said.

Schulman's analysis scrambles familiar ideological lines. She looks askance at trigger warnings; she also looks askance at Zionism. She considers the way accusations of sexual threat have been used against Black and queer people and then uses that understanding to extend empathy to those accused of sexual harassment. She tries to dissect the internal logic of police brutality and domestic abuse. Her ideas' appeal lies in offering a new way to consider seemingly intractable problems and in drawing lines between our political ideals and the way we behave in daily life. ("There are a lot of progressive people who are very petty," Schulman told me. "So what kind of progressive world can they build?") They're complicated ideas, and the book takes them in directions sure to give every reader something to disagree with. But—at least within the realm of personal relationships—they also come down to an almost kindergartenishly simple dictum: Talk, listen, work things out.

As she makes clear, this directive is simple but hardly easy. One of the reasons so many people claim victimhood is that, in Schulman's observation, having your pain taken seriously is a gift only victims seem to receive. "It's about being eligible for compassion," she told me. "But everybody deserves support, regardless of what position they're in."

Schulman began writing *Conflict Is Not Abuse* in 2014, during a summer shadowed by the death of Michael Brown in Ferguson, by the death of Eric Garner on Staten Island, and by the deaths of some two thousand Palestinians in Gaza. These events seemed to her to share a form. Soon, she was talking with her students about Garner; she was having long arguments on Facebook about Israel; she was angry about what she saw as terrible injustices, but she was also interested in how they came to be. How did a violent cop or a member of the Israeli army rationalize what he or she had done? Listening to the explanations on offer suggested that anxiety and fear had given rise to a "mortal overreaction by an oppressive force," Schulman told me. The cops and Israeli soldiers had seen themselves as victims and lashed out.

The results, in those cases, were fatal. But Schulman began to recognize the same pattern playing out in her private life: a misplaced sense of danger, an overreaction, then a rift that came to seem impossible to repair. Two friends would have a fight, then one would persuade the rest of their clique to turn on the other. Someone would express a dissenting opinion, then face accusations of violence and calls for punishment. Schulman saw people turning away from the challenges of conflict and instead asking some larger body—a group of friends, a college bureaucracy, the state—to ratify their status as victims and intervene on their behalf.

"A nonfiction book is the story of an idea," Schulman told me—and the analysis found in *Conflict Is Not Abuse*, she writes, brings "fifty-seven years of living and thirty-five years of writing to a critical conclusion." In this case, the idea's story is perhaps also her own.

Schulman's family lived on 10th Street when she was born, in 1958; she lives on 9th Street now, and when we first met, in very early March, it was at a boutique hotel on Eighth. She has a soft face, a deliberate cadence, and wry wit. Of her status as a fixture in the neighborhood, "the only thing older than me is Veselka," she said. (The restaurant opened in 1954.)

Schulman has stayed close to where she was born but not because it was ever an easy place to be. Growing up Jewish and middle-class in Manhattan, she came from what she has called a Holocaust family, with a history "typical of my Jewish generation: soaked in blood, trauma, and dislocation." It was also a family in which, she has said, "being a smart female was an insurmountable problem and being gay was the ultimate disaster."

In *Conflict Is Not Abuse*, she describes going to her high-school guidance counselor for help: "I was sixteen in 1975 and faced the brutality of my parents' homophobia," she writes. In response, the counselor "told me not to tell my classmates that I was a lesbian because they could shun me." After graduation, she left the city for the University of Chicago, but she soon returned to attend Hunter College, where she studied with Audre Lorde. By 1979, she was working as a reporter for the city's underground queer press and waitressing at a coffee shop in Tribeca.

While waiting tables, she managed to write and publish two books, but some of the neighborhood artists who were her regulars suggested it might be useful to get an MFA. She enrolled in a City College writing program taught by Grace Paley, and on the first day, she read aloud an excerpt from her current project—her third novel, which had a lesbian narrator. The other students assumed the narrator was a man. Paley asked Schulman to come to her office after class. "Look, you're really a writer," Schulman remembered Paley telling her. "You don't need this class. Go home." She dropped out.

That third novel, *After Delores*, was a noirish detective story narrated by a lesbian waitress, and it garnered Schulman's first book review in the *New York Times*. ("I read the book, found the lady sleuth to be a vomit-stained, coffee-stained, bloodstained lesbian with great self-doubt and a rather severe hygiene problem, and decided I liked it," wrote the cowboy singer and writer Kinky Friedman in his enthusiastic review.)

In the eighties, Schulman was finding success and also finding a community: a downtown world of queer artists and leftists throwing parties and forming ad hoc political groups and collaborating on projects—like the New York Lesbian & Gay Experimental Film Festival, which Schulman started in 1987 with filmmaker Jim Hubbard. "We were sitting in her apartment smoking a joint," Hubbard recalled. "Sarah handed me the joint and said, 'We should do a lesbian and gay experimental-film festival.' And I said, 'I've always wanted to. When should we do it?' And Sarah thought for a little bit and said, 'September.'" The festival (now called MIX NYC) went on to host the first New York screening of *Paris Is Burning* and early work by Todd Haynes.

Even as that community was flourishing creatively, it faced the devastation of a plague. Schulman and her peers watched friends and lovers die terrible deaths from AIDS as powerful institutions mostly shrugged. The scale of mainstream indifference to the plight of AIDS victims makes comparison with, say, the current coronavirus pandemic difficult. This was not a disease that most Americans saw as a crisis that had anything to do with them. "Why Make AIDS Worse than It Is?" read the headline of one *New York Times* editorial. "The disease is still very largely confined to specific risk groups. Once all susceptible members are infected, the numbers of new victims will decline."

That indifference galvanized a generation of activists. The same year Schulman and Hubbard founded their film festival, Larry Kramer spurred the founding of ACT UP. Schulman and Hubbard both joined. ACT UP members infiltrated the New York Stock Exchange, where they chained themselves to a balcony and disrupted the opening bell; they shut down FDA headquarters; they covered Jesse Helms's house in a giant condom. The group's combative spirit remains bracing. When Kramer died in May, the *Times* still seemed disturbed by the force of his rage. "He worked hard to shock the country into dealing with AIDS as a public health emergency," read the subheading of his obituary. "But his often-abusive approach could overshadow his achievements." In this context, however, being "confrontational" (a word the *Times* later swapped in for "abusive") was not a quirk of personality; it was the point. And between the federal government (or the *New York Times*) and Larry Kramer, which party was really in a position to "abuse" the other? Indeed, remarked one observer on Twitter, "calling Larry Kramer 'abusive' is actually an ancient mystic ritual to summon Sarah Schulman."

Schulman is devoted to preserving the memory of the ACT UP era and of the hard work that its accomplishments required. In June 2001, she and Hubbard began the ACT UP Oral History Project, for which they recorded interviews with more than 180 surviving members of the group. Hubbard and filmmaker James Wentzy filmed, and she asked questions. "She would be in this intense relationship with the other person—a little bit like therapy," Hubbard said.

The oral histories have also become the basis for Schulman's next book, which Farrar, Straus and Giroux will publish in 2021. Her approach to the material is at once unsentimental and resolutely personal. As she writes in her Oral History statement, the project calls on the same sense of responsibility with which she'd been raised to regard the Holocaust: for remembering the dead, identifying the perpetrators, and "refusing revisionism" in a story of mass death. Her new book will push against the view of ACT UP as an organization of primarily affluent white gay men.

Over the years, Schulman has been wary of the way queer stories tend to enter the mainstream—homogenized and flattering to straight audiences—and has argued forcefully against the diminishment she sees. "People are talking about some remarkable similarities between the hit musical [*Rent*] and Sarah Schulman's novel *People in Trouble*," read a 1997 item in this magazine. That 1990 book concerned an AIDS-era love triangle among queer New York artists and activists; the non-Puccini portions of the 1996 musical bear a clear resemblance to the novel, both in the outlines of relationships and in specific plot points. The crucial difference, of course, is that in the book, the queer characters are the center of the story, where in Jonathan Larson's musical, they're pushed to the side. "Schulman is angrier about the depiction in *Rent* of gay people and the AIDS crisis than any allegedly lifted material," wrote the reporter. The musical sent the message that "straight people are the heroic center of the AIDS crisis," Schulman told him. (The episode became the kernel of her 1998 book, *Stagestruck*, on the recent commodification of queer culture.)

The Lesbian Avengers, a group Schulman cofounded in 1992, carried the oppositional spirit of ACT UP in new directions. The journalist and City College professor Linda Villarosa recalled finding herself in Schulman's social circle in those years: "I remember her being so smart, so intense—you know, somebody who just really stuck to their guns and made things happen." Things like the Dyke March: an annual permit-free protest march ahead of official Pride events, orchestrated by the Lesbian Avengers and staged in New York for the first time in 1993. "I was like, 'What? A human being can just do that?'" Villarosa said. "You could decide that lesbians were going to take over part of the street? Be topless?"

As queer people were increasingly invited to identify with mainstream power in the nineties and aughts—as gay rights gained purchase, as Pride went corporate—new questions arose. The movement from outsider to insider, to identifying with power, presents a crucial turn in *Conflict Is Not Abuse*. How might people who were once oppressed then become oppressors? For Schulman, this reckoning arrived in 2009, when she was invited to give a talk at Tel Aviv University about *Ties That Bind*, her book on familial homophobia. A friend told her she couldn't go—there was a boycott. What boycott? Schulman wondered. "So I started to find out about it, and I realized that I couldn't go."

She declined the invitation and began to examine how she'd come to this pass. "I had to face all the prejudices I'd been raised with," she told me. Having grown up with the specter of the Holocaust, she confronted the possibility that Jews, having been victims, might now be perpetrators as well—and that, in fact, the ways that they'd been victims in the past might blind them to their own power to abuse. "I came to this very, very late, and I feel very badly about that," she said. "At some point, if you want to have a real life, you have to say, 'I did that then, this is why I did it, but I don't have to do it.' It's possible to do that. You don't have to be a martyr or a saint to do that."

The subtitle of *Conflict Is Not Abuse* is *Overstating Harm, Community Responsibility, and the Duty of Repair*. The last of those three phrases is one Schulman also uses in *The Cosmopolitans*—the novel she published the same year as *Conflict Is Not Abuse*. Set in the 1950s, it centers on two friends in New York City who have lived next door to each other for thirty years. "I know there is cruelty in life," *The Cosmopolitans'* heroine says. "But I believe that it can be followed by reconciliation." She says she believes "in the duty of repair." Life in a family, in a community, in a place like New York City, seems to demand a belief that repair and resolution are possible, and that their pursuit is necessary, if we're all going to keep living together.

Perhaps Schulman's most provocative move in *Conflict Is Not Abuse* is her insistence that overstatement of harm happens everywhere: People in power who face criticism can overstate harm, but people who have previously suffered—who have lived through real harm—can do it too. For those in positions of dominance, she told me, "opposition feels like an attack." Meanwhile, for those who have survived trauma, "it's sometimes so hard to just keep it together that being asked to be self-critical can feel like your whole world is going to fall apart." The explanation is different, but the result can be similar.

For readers focused on establishing the gravity and reality of domestic abuse, Schulman's critical scrutiny of the term's use may seem counterproductive. Her broader point, though, is that we live in "a culture of underreaction to abuse and overreaction to conflict," as she writes. "Abuse" happens in situations where one person has direct power over the other; her analysis of "conflict" concerns situations of mutual participation, or in which the powerful person is in denial.

These distinctions may be clearer in Schulman's telling than in real life, where the question of who has power (A pop star? A music critic? The pop star's army of online fans?) can prove more elusive than one would hope. At the same time, Schulman's refusal to flatten human experience into politically useful platitudes—she doubts, for example, that "no" always means "no"—will alarm some readers no matter what.

Even before the book was published, it was subject to a backlash on Tumblr. "People were furious about this book," the writer and podcaster merritt k told me. "Just the title sparked so much outrage. People saw *Conflict Is Not Abuse* and basically thought, *Oh, this is someone telling me that I wasn't abused.*" A friend and fan of Schulman's, she took to Goodreads, writing a positive if measured review. "Many of the examples Schulman describes resonated with me, also a queer woman, but they may ring hollow to those outside these communities," she allowed.

Schulman believes that those who read her book as denying their own experiences of abuse are misunderstanding her, but she also seems interested in the defensiveness the book provokes. She heard from one reader who was upset that *Conflict Is Not Abuse* "made her question whether the partner she had accused of being abusive really was abusive," she told me. "She saw that as an assault, that it made her doubt herself."

Rankine told me that she and Schulman talked a lot about the title of the book and the question of whether conflict itself might at a certain point become abusive. "I felt our position on that is different," she said. "I do feel like there's a moment when you can't really put yourself in that position again—to be in a position of conflict willingly, because the trauma and abuse is too much." She acknowledged a kind of utopian strain in her friend's thinking. "Sarah is committed to action—things becoming newly formed," she said. "In that way, I think she's a greater optimist than I am."

Surely, progress for broken people and broken countries demands some belief in the possibility of repair. Schulman's analysis of our political straits doesn't come with a to-do list of actions for directly tackling the structural problems she recognizes. She warns that we enhance state power when we call the police, but she doesn't prescribe how to attack it at the root. Seeing why a violent cop might behave the way he does is one thing; getting that cop to understand his own behavior with enlightened self-awareness is a greater challenge.

A more serious criticism, then, might have to do with practical application of *Conflict Is Not Abuse*. Reading Schulman's book is invigorating: It offers the experience of reconsidering the world around you and bumping up against habits of mind you didn't realize you had. It's hard to imagine finishing it without feeling some pang of uncomfortable recognition or without reliving that pang the next time you are tempted to take one of the shortcuts she abhors—joining in when friends bemoan a loathed ex, ignoring a text instead of picking up the phone to make things right.

But people take shortcuts for a reason. Even before you arrive at the obstacles to solving problems like state violence, where implementing her theories is hard to imagine, just upholding Schulman's ideals within the personal sphere is a daunting task. "The social world she's describing is *so time consuming*," her friend Lana Dee Povitz told me. It demands constant self-scrutiny, ongoing dialogue, diligent fact-finding, and availability for intervention in the personal lives of one's friends. "That world she's asking for is nearly impossible under capitalism," Povitz said.

Povitz was a twenty-six-year-old living in a queer collective in Brooklyn when she met Schulman. It was 2012. Povitz was part of a group of twenty-somethings just learning how to organize—they wanted to fight gentrification—and she ran a book club that was reading Schulman's 2012 book, *Gentrification of the Mind*. After Povitz got in touch about reproducing some material, Schulman volunteered to come speak to her group.

Schulman wanted to start by hearing about them; she was curious about their lives and their work. She asked questions. She listened. And she asked more. *Did they know their neighbors?* Povitz remembered Schulman asking. *Did they help with the neighbors' kids? Did they know the local churches? Did they know what work the churches were already doing?*

"We were just like, 'No, no, no, no, we don't,'" Povitz told me. "'Oh my God, we don't.'"

Schulman "doesn't do a lot of the feminine niceties that a lot of women seem trained to perform," Povitz said—things like the agreeable smiling and mirroring that smooth over mild social disjuncture and keep conversations rolling comfortably along. Instead of, say, offering gentle encouragement, Schulman made it plain how deeply "unimpressive" she found the group's efforts. They were not doing the things Schulman believed necessary to make a material difference in others' lives, so she said so. "It was kind of devastating," Povitz recalled.

Today, Povitz teaches at Middlebury; she's a historian of US social movements, and she often assigns Schulman's work. When we spoke, she was still audibly pained by the memory of their first encounter. Povitz remembered that plenty of people were upset: They were self-conscious, they got defensive, they found Schulman to be "mean and blunt." But Povitz also saw something else. "There were people who were really put off," she said. "And then there were people who were like, *This is hard, and I want to sit with it.*" The people in the group who were willing to sit with criticism, who could hear unflattering opinions and have difficult conversations—"those were the people I knew I wanted to identify with politically," she said. That willingness was valuable, Povitz realized, even if it was rare.

Upon meeting her new editor at FSG, Jackson Howard, Schulman told me, she made an immediate request. "The first day I was like, 'Treat me like a sixty-year-old man,'" she said. "And he did!" Since then, their relationship has been "great."

Howard laughed when I asked if he remembered the exchange. He said he was "probably trembling" at the time. Howard is twenty-six, and he'd admired Schulman's work since reading *After Delores* in a college class called Bad Homosexuals—but it was more than that. "Sarah has a reputation for being a hard-ass," he recalled of his impression before that first breakfast meeting. "Even in her writing, she is uncompromising. She is cutthroat. She does not back down from her positions." He sought to win her trust, knowing that he represented the kind of institution that traditionally had not been on her side. "I mean, she is somebody who's made a career out of conflict and out of confrontation and out of provocation—but never for the sake of doing it."

In this sense, *Conflict Is Not Abuse* is "a really good window into her," Villarosa told me. "I think she wants to tell you, 'It's okay for us to have conflicts.'" Perhaps the need for reassurance is somewhat generational. "In the nineties, that was big—in ACT UP, people were just coming to blows, practically, and I think now people are more afraid of conflict than we were back then."

Schulman's comfort with conflict is well known. (In 2005, she was the subject of a write-up in the *Times* with the headline "Who's Afraid of Sarah Schulman?" that now reads as arguably sexist and startlingly snide.) "I think what people don't as much understand about her is that she's very kind," Villarosa said. She is a frequent dinner guest at Schulman's home, where meals are planned generously and guests' assistance is refused. "You schlep up however many floors to get to her place in that tiny apartment," Villarosa told me. "Her bedroom is an inch away from the living room, you know, but it's like a salon, going to her house, because there will always be a couple of other smart people over there."

The last time Villarosa was over, it was Lydia Polgreen and Rankine. (Rankine and Schulman also talk on the phone every Sunday.) Schulman once hosted Villarosa's mother after she and Linda debated whether queer people are inevitably let down by their families; Villarosa had insisted (contra Schulman's convictions about familial homophobia) that her mother was one of her best friends. Sometime later, Schulman asked Villarosa whether she could invite "Mrs. V" to dinner. Mrs. V and Schulman had a lovely time and talked at length about the theater. "She just loves to get people in a room to talk about ideas and to sit and help her expand her mind," said Villarosa. "And also to give her opinions, and I really, really appreciate that about her."

"My experience is that she's interested in the thing that is interesting to you," said Matt Brim, a friend who, like Schulman, teaches at CUNY's College of Staten Island. "She wants to know how you're thinking about it. She wants to encourage you to think as well as you can about the thing you're thinking about." A few years ago, Schulman invited Villarosa to give a lecture about the reporting she'd done on HIV/AIDS over the years. "She has such high standards, so I wanted to do a really good job," Villarosa said. She went back to her earliest work for *Essence* in the eighties and carried through to the present, describing the ongoing danger of HIV/AIDS for gay and bisexual Black men in the South. Schulman found the material arresting. After the lecture, "she sat me down and she said, 'This is really important. You need to do something else with this.'" Villarosa had assumed what she was saying was familiar; Schulman was adamant that it was news. "And that became my first cover story for the *New York Times Magazine*," Villarosa said.

merritt k told me she saw *Conflict Is Not Abuse* as most valuable within small communities—queer communities, radical communities, whose members can't afford to turn on one another. For them, it conveyed a message that "hey, guys, if we're running around trying to take each other out constantly, that's not a good place to be." Before the lockdown, merritt would go over to Schulman's apartment every few months. There, Schulman would pour her a glass of whiskey and they'd talk about what they each were working on. "I don't know if she would like this," merritt said, "but I kind of think of her as my queer mom."

For Schulman, the classroom is a microcosm where it's possible to apply the book's principles on a manageable scale. "In a healthy educational forum," she writes in *Conflict Is Not Abuse*, "students engage materials regardless of agreement or comfort level and then analyze, debate, critique, and learn from them, addressing the discomfort as well as the text." For this reason, in the classroom, she has a "no censorship" rule. "Students can engage any subject, event, or character and use any language that they feel is appropriate," she writes. "Any student who has criticism, insight, or objection to these elements has the equal right to express their views in detail. This has been my policy for sixteen years without a single complaint."

Schulman often teaches a Friday-night fiction class from 6:30 to 10. "So my students have worked all week, they've taken care of their kids, and they're coming to write fiction on Friday night," she said. With the pandemic, her students' challenges are more apparent than ever. "Their children are home from school, their parents are unemployed, they don't have good Wi-Fi, and also they don't always want their families to hear what their class discussions are like," she told me.

She has found that teaching at a working-class institution like hers can clarify the debates of campus culture. "No one has ever asked for a trigger warning," she said. "It's a very entitled position to believe that you have the right and the ability to control other people." When she visits other schools, the contrast is stark. She told me she remembered an exchange that followed a talk she once gave at Columbia. "There was a girl there who was Black, and she was from Queens, and she was saying, 'In my neighborhood, I was taught to be resilient. And then I come to Columbia, and they say you should be protected. Which is better? Resilient or protected?'" For Schulman, the answer was obvious.

"I was like, 'Resilient!'"

As she was writing the book, she did not expect trigger warnings or "cancel culture" to become focal points of discussion.

"I didn't even really know about cancel culture," Schulman told me. "I didn't know the phrase." But her talks and readings from the book drew the largest audiences of her career; the crowds were young, "and that's what they wanted to talk about." Now she sees a document like the recent "Letter on Justice and Open Debate" published in *Harper's* as a "classic example," she said, of the dynamic she described in her book: People from a "dominant culture feel threatened" and are reacting as if danger is afoot.

"The idea of free speech is being co-opted by the right," she told me. "The answer is more speech, not less." The risk of trying to limit speech, in her view, is that limitations will always be turned against the most vulnerable first. She pointed to the tendency to link speech in defense of Palestinians with anti-Semitism—a rhetorical move favored by, for example, Cary Nelson and Bari Weiss, who numbered among the signatories of the *Harper's* letter. (Last year, Weiss was photographed at home, a copy of *Conflict Is Not Abuse* visible on her shelf. She told me she had not read the book and that it was a gift.)

When Schulman and I first spoke in early March, she was optimistic about "the big-tent movement" the Bernie Sanders campaign looked poised to assemble. "Well, you know," she said when we spoke this summer, "there is a big-tent coalition in the street." In the months since, the world had by most accounts fallen apart, fragmenting in ways that appeared shocking even as the pattern of the fault lines was familiar. "Victimhood" and "threat" were terms once again up for grabs—as federal agents turned tear gas on peaceful protesters, as entrenched elites ran for cover. Collective failures of communication and understanding—on matters as seemingly innocuous as germ theory—became more apparent and more dire.

Nearly four years after publishing a book that argued strenuously against calling the police, Schulman was pleased to see more people coming around to the idea. And the spasms of self-scrutiny shaking institutions across the country struck her as a somewhat predictable turn of events. "They wanted to bring in people of color and keep the organization the same—and that's an unreasonable demand," she said. "If the demand is that every cultural institution should be controlled by people of color, I'm fine with that."

A lifetime of activism has left her with a complex appreciation for the practical matter of demands. "I'm very concretely focused," she said. "I like when movements have reasonable, winnable, and doable demands and build campaigns toward them. But those kinds of movements are the most successful when they're also simultaneously utopian movements." The spirit that animates Schulman's work, a sense of risk and possibility in difference, seems all the more urgent now—and all the more difficult to conjure. "The fact that something could go wrong does not mean we are in danger," as she writes in the first chapter of *Conflict Is Not Abuse*. "It means that we are alive."

Sarah Schulman Discusses Her Massive ACT UP Tome *Let the Record Show*, Coming This May

Tim Murphy / 2021

Originally published in *TheBody*, April 13, 2021. Reprinted with permission of Myles Helfand and Remedy Health Media.

It's fascinating to watch how traumatic and fraught events get historicized, isn't it? Think the Holocaust. Think the Vietnam War. And think the US 1980s and nineties AIDS crisis and the furious activism that rose up to meet it. Only in the past decade have we started seeing major nonfiction works of film or publishing take on that seismic era (which, we should point out, is not over). First, we had David France's Oscar-nominated 2012 documentary *How to Survive a Plague*, centered on ACT UP New York, and, a few years later, his massive book of the same title, a more detailed account with a strong focus on HIV drug development, less so on the societal side of AIDS such as drug use, homelessness, and racial inequities.

And soon, starting May 18, we'll have *Let the Record Show: A Political History of ACT UP New York, 1987–1993*. The twentieth title from acclaimed author, activist, and ACT UP alum Sarah Schulman, the book is the culmination of twenty years' worth of in-depth video interviews with nearly two hundred ACT UP alums. Organized not chronologically, like France's book, but by ACT UP's myriad campaigns and subgroups, the book is an exhaustive compendium of oral history, bound together by Schulman's insights into what made ACT UP unique among activist movements, why and how it both succeeded and failed, and what modern-day movements can learn from it.

As an avowed ACT UP junkie, I devoured *Let the Record Show* in a few weeks, despite its massiveness. Never before, including in the documentary film *United in Anger*, has ACT UP been portrayed with such multifaceted, granular attention to how each and every major campaign played out. It's less a Schulman polemic and score-settler than a deeply generous platform for nearly every ACT UP member's personal story, motives, and recollections to be told in one place, adding up to an enthralling mosaic of biography, collaboration, and, often, conflict. It's often funny and deeply moving, thanks to both Schulman's voice and the many others she orchestrates here. As Schulman herself pointed out on the call, it's a "yearbook" of sorts for the hundreds, if not thousands, of people from disparate backgrounds who came together at a particular time and place to fight back in a time of profound terror and frustration. And it's an intriguing but plainspoken dissection of what makes movements work, or fall apart, at a time when the work ACT UP did some thirty years ago seems at once impossibly difficult (no cell phones, email, or internet!) and also impossible to imagine getting away with today, including public figures who were actually shamable and federal buildings that were easily breached.

The Body talked with Schulman about her magnum opus, how she constructed it, and what purpose she wants it to serve in the world.

Tim Murphy: Hi, Sarah! Congratulations on finishing this massive tome. So first of all, I wanted to ask, in the book's final pages, you reveal that in recent years, you have been struggling with a health condition. How are you doing now?

Sarah Schulman: Yes. I found out I have the JAK2 gene, a somatic mutation where your cells multiply too quickly—a very bizarre, weird thing. It started when I had a yoga accident. They took an X-ray and said, "Oh my God, you have a huge lesion on your bone—you have bone cancer." I was like, *what*? They opened my shoulder and found there was a huge clot there. A few years later, I was having trouble breathing and they found out I had ten blood clots in my lungs. I also had to have surgeries on my legs. I have a better grip on it now, but it requires permanent, constant maintenance. I take a low dose of chemo every day. I'm in stage 2, and stage 4 is leukemia, but my progression is really slow, so I just might get away with it.

But then again, who could be better prepared for this than me? A strange illness that the patient has to figure out by reading medical journals and figuring out clinical trials. It was all incredibly familiar. And then at NYU I have an older nurse who started there in the 1980s, and we end up talking about AIDS, these two little old ladies . . .

Murphy: Right, and of course as I read about it, and even your extreme difficulty walking down the street and getting up the stairs in your apartment building, one cannot help but think of what so many people in the East Village, where you live, went through in the 1980s and nineties with AIDS. It was a strange, poignant echo of the whole book. Well, glad to hear you've got it somewhat under control now, so let's talk about the book. How long in total did you work on it?

Schulman: It really started when Jim Hubbard and I started the ACT UP Oral History Project in 2001 and over the next eighteen years did interviews with 188 surviving ACT UP members. In the nineties, the internet revolution eclipsed ACT UP—nothing from ACT UP was digitized—so when people started going on the internet, there was nothing there. People writing dissertations on ACT UP and AIDS activism were using the *New York Times* for their sources, coming away with the idea that, you know, "At first Americans had problems with people with AIDS, but then they came around." And Jim and I thought, "This cannot be the way that this story will be told."

So we started interviewing people and making the interviews available. We asked for $25,000 in funding from the Ford Foundation, but at the time, [longtime LGBTQ activist] Urvashi Vaid was working there. She asked us to rewrite the grant and gave us $300,000, so this was really her vision. The money went to everything—the camera, software, transcriptions, the website, broadband, office space, travel.

Only a few people refused interviews. Then Jim collected two thousand hours of archival footage, on all sorts of different formats.

Murphy: Right, which led to your 2012 ACT UP documentary *United in Anger*. So then why the book, too?

Schulman: We put all this archival stuff out there, and no [writer] really did anything with it, analyzed it to see the tropes that were revealed. So finally I wrote a proposal, and FSG [the publisher Farrar, Straus and Giroux] bought it.

Murphy: So the book is structured not in a traditionally chronological story but more by theme—ACT UP's big campaigns or facets, such as drug development, expanding the official definition of AIDS to include women-only symptoms, needle exchange, housing for homeless people living with HIV, the Latino movements within ACT UP, the art and video work within ACT UP. Why that structure?

Schulman: I felt like if I told it the traditional way, you wouldn't get the true story. I started going through the interviews and noting tropes or themes every time I would see them. So, for example, there are three sections on Latino involvement in ACT UP because there were actually three

Latino movements. I wanted to show the depth. And I decided to end it in 1993 because I didn't want to end it with the "happy ending" of protease inhibitors arriving in 1996. Because [even though ACT UP never disbanded and is still active today, as she notes at the start of the book], a particular era of ACT UP ended in 1993, and I wanted to show how crazy and desperate everyone was at that point, organizing political funerals and riding around in vans with the bodies of their dead friends. I wanted to convey what the suffering was like at that point.

Murphy: How do you feel about having finally finished the book?

Schulman: I'm proud of how fair it is. People in and out of ACT UP have had a lot of anxiety about this book, thinking, "Oh, she's gonna bitch slap the white gay men who were in ACT UP," but that's not what it is at all. I did this book in a fair way that's not oriented toward nostalgia but toward people who want to make change right now.

Murphy: So if you had to boil down this massive tome, what would you say are the takeaway messages you want to get across as the book comes out into the world soon?

Schulman: One thing is that ACT UP's greatest achievement by far was forcing the CDC to change its definition of AIDS [to include symptoms experienced primarily by women, which opened up women to disability benefits, more research opportunities, etc.]. ACT UP fought for that for four years and finally won. And as [fellow activist] Terry McGovern says, if you look at AIDS timelines, you'll see Rock Hudson but never when they expanded the CDC definition.

Message #2 is that people pick political strategies based on their social position. Because Larry Kramer went to Yale with the head of [drugmaker] BMS, he could bring people like [ACT UP alum and then Treatment Action Group founder] Mark Harrington to a catered lunch at BMS. But it took the women in the group two years to get meetings [with government and pharma officials]. Then you take the wildest group of all in ACT UP, the drug users. They were messy, but they also won [the right to legal needle exchange in New York City]. So whoever you are, you can win, but you have to work much harder and be messier if you don't have access to power.

Message #3 is that perfect consensus does not work—and that's important to know now, because we're in a time that's extremely moralistic with an emphasis on homogeneity of analysis, strategy, and language. What works is what ACT UP did, which was to create a big tent, a radical democracy in which people are allowed to respond from where they're at. If your movement facilitates what people need to do, you have a better chance of succeeding.

Murphy: Can you give an example of what you mean by our current times?

Schulman: I mean that theoryism is irrelevant. Your theory should emerge from your actions, which then reveal your values. Take the current argument: "Lesbians are disappearing because so many people are becoming trans[gender]." That's idiotic. The question is: People who actually exist, do they have rights? And if they don't, how do you protect them? That's what matters, not endless battles about theoretical positionings. What are people's real material living conditions? When you're running a campaign, you want to make demands that are reasonable, winnable, and doable. ACT UP presented solutions [to people in power], and when [those people] said no, ACT UP did nonviolent civil disobedience to force them to listen and accommodate. That's so much better than begging authorities from an infantilized position to solve your problems.

And also, a coalition is not a Benetton ad where you have, like, one Latino and one Black person. It's where you have silos of like-minded people who are working together effectively.

So all of these pieces of information, I think, are essential for people who are doing work today, and are the central arguments of the book.

Murphy: What was the hardest part of writing the book?

Schulman: How to deal with the dead people. There are so many people I never got to interview. How to evoke them.

Murphy: Meaning how to be honest about them but still respectful?

Schulman: Meaning how to represent people who were very influential and beloved. So I tried to replicate the experience of death in ACT UP, which was that sometimes your best friend died and sometimes someone died who you'd only seen once. So that's why each chapter ends with an "In Memoriam" [survivors' memories of late comrades], to reflect that.

I also had to figure out the art side of ACT UP. Because, at the time, if you looked at galleries, you saw white people, but if you looked at nightlife, you saw people of color.

Murphy: What was the most rewarding part?

Schulman: The photos—so many that nobody's ever seen, such as the Latino Caucus in Puerto Rico at the time and then their thirtieth reunion photo. Or seeing [the late] Katrina Haslip with Terry McGovern, who looks like she's five at the time but was actually twenty-nine.

Murphy: In all your years archiving and historicizing ACT UP, long after you'd actually been in it, did your feelings about it evolve?

Schulman: Definitely. Most people in ACT UP only knew what they and their friends in the group did. They think that that was the center. So to create this overview was a real accomplishment. The big question I was trying to answer was: What do all these different people have in common? Was everyone raised with some sense of community? But that didn't pan out. We thought it might be everyone having had a traumatic experience with AIDS. No. People came to ACT UP who did not know anyone with AIDS. It was only in Year 8, when I was interviewing Rebecca Cole, an actress who came to ACT UP with no ties to AIDS, that I realized: "Oh. Coming to ACT UP is not based on an experience. These are people who cannot be bystanders."

Murphy: But of course there were people who came to ACT UP primarily motivated to save their and their friends' and loved ones' own lives. Peter Staley has said he probably never would've left Wall Street, come out of the closet, and joined ACT UP if he hadn't been diagnosed HIV positive.

Schulman: But plenty of people like Peter never came to ACT UP. Most PWAs [people living with AIDS] never did anything [activistic].

Murphy: One thing that really stood out for me was how many people in ACT UP—not all, but many—had gone to very elite schools. Yale, Oberlin, Wesleyan, Harvard, etc. Why do you think so?

Schulman: It's true that the elite Whitney Museum Study Program was a big feeder into ACT UP of many of the art and video people. But overall I don't think the elitism is that overwhelming. Many people were coming from working- or middle-class backgrounds even if they went on to elite schools. People who go to those fancy schools are more likely to tell you so. Also, this was New York—it attracts ambitious climbers with dreams.

Murphy: You say early on in the book that you were a "rank and file" ACT UP member—never leadership. Why so?

Schulman: I didn't really identify that much with the people there. I was doing a lot of other things. I was writing novels. I had already been active in the women's reproductive rights movement and was brought into ACT UP by Maxine Wolfe. But I went to the Monday meetings and the major actions, and was arrested twice. There were a thousand people like me [who were members but not lead organizers].

But I went to ACT UP because it was effective. Maxine and I had been kicked out of the reproductive rights movement in a lesbian purge, and that was painful. I realized that, in ACT UP, I would never be kicked out because of homophobia. And they had resources. I'd work a table for ACT UP and people would just hand over $20 bills. They had men's money. You could do a lot more. It was privilege and principle meeting in the same room for the first time.

Murphy: Did you have a favorite campaign in ACT UP? Was it the women's CDC definition campaign?

Schulman: That's the most important by far. But I also loved the creative things that the Action Tours [ACT UP affinity, or breakout, group] did, like the "Santa Has HIV" action at the holidays.

Murphy: I love how you tell us in the book who people were and what they were doing at the moment they came into ACT UP—an artist, a Wall Street broker, women with AIDS coming right out of prison, etc. What about you? Who were you in 1987?

Schulman: I was twenty-eight, someone who'd already been covering AIDS [for publications including the *Village Voice* and the *New York Native*] since 1982, so I had opinions and information and movement experience. I was impressed that women came into leadership so quickly in ACT UP. People were so desperate that they would actually listen to lesbians.

Murphy: Much of the book is told as verbatim oral history, but I still found concerning a few instances where someone makes an allegation of someone and it does not appear that you went to that other person, among the surviving people, and asked them for comment. Such as someone saying that [filmmaker] Jennie Livingston kicked out her HIV-positive roommate [the late] Ray Navarro because he had TB, or Charles King saying that Larry Kramer [who died only last year] made racist, or at least "racially insensitive," statements on the ACT UP floor.

Schulman: I didn't ask any [of those alleged against] to comment. I just took the interviews. And those things are true, believe me.

Murphy: That's not the point—it's that you didn't ask those people to comment, to defend themselves.

Schulman: Sorry, I'm not agreeing with you on that.

Murphy: Fair enough. So I wanted to ask you what you thought of David Dinkins, who was mayor 1989 to 1993, a big chunk of your book's span. How would you rate him on AIDS?

Schulman: He appointed the city's first LGBT liaison, Marjorie Hill. But he was a frightened guy who was scared of everything, including needle exchange. Can we talk about Anthony Fauci, though? This book was submitted before the second coming of Anthony Fauci [as a COVID hero]. But in this book, every time he is mentioned, it's somebody saying, "We went to him and asked him to do something, and he said no." Parallel track [to allow more people with HIV into otherwise rigid drug trials], IV drug users—over and over, he said no. It was only when we forced him by major embarrassing actions such as breaking into his agency's offices, that he changed. The fact that he's since been reconstructed as the hero of AIDS is kind of crazy.

Murphy: And I wanted to ask you about just that, because it seems as though many of ACT UP's successes hinged on the fact that people in power could still be shamed, publicly exposed as negligent or indifferent. All the shaming in the world did little to stop Trump and his enablers, the past four years. Do you think shaming as a political tool has lost its power?

Schulman: Well, I would put it differently. I don't like the word shaming. I would say resistance. Take Larry Kramer. The best thing about him was that he was a rich man with a lot of connections, and he yelled at those people. And that's what did not happen in the Republican Party the past four years. People with access to power have to give up their personal ambition and risk alienating people in power by talking to them honestly in a public way.

Murphy: I was very struck in your book by the subdrama of Derek Link, an ACT UP member who for years told other, HIV-positive members of the group that he, too, was HIV positive, but in fact wasn't. Perpetuating such a Rachel Dolezal-like fraud would seem to be grounds for cancellation from his peers, but I did notice on Facebook that all his friends and loving commenters are many, many fellow ACT UP alums.

Schulman: That's ACT UP. People are very bonded. People who disagreed about everything still love each other, because we did this thing together and made a difference, and there's very few people who can say that. I don't even look at Derek as a fraud. I think there was a lot of trauma and he thought it was inevitable that he was going to get AIDS. Quite a few people in ACT UP or AIDS activism or work seroconverted much later.

Murphy: You spend a lot of time in the book on the tensions that led to about twelve people, the treatment wonks, leaving ACT UP and starting the more private Treatment Action Group [TAG], which would meet privately with pharma and government officials like Fauci. And many people have said that this was the end of a powerful era for ACT UP, even though of course the group continued on, and though some people were in both TAG and ACT UP. And you really give everyone their voice on the split and some of the tense things that led up to it, and you say that you yourself remained agnostic. But let me ask you: How might things have played out if they hadn't left?

Schulman: I think [the treatment wonks] would've had to adjust the way they were doing things. If they had stayed and said, "We really do care about women with AIDS [the treatment wonks were seen as this not being a focus of theirs] and equal access, but we also have strong feelings about what we want to pursue, so let's reorganize so we can address this . . ." then

I think ACT UP's next strong campaign would've been the fight for universal health care [which many in the group had prioritized]. But everyone in the group was crazy by that point, and I think it might've been too much to ask. Maybe if we'd all had good therapy, we could have evolved into a health care movement.

Murphy: Let me ask you another theoretical. What if, from about 1987 on, there hadn't been an ACT UP? How might things have played out?

Schulman: There wouldn't have been needle exchange or housing for homeless people with AIDS in New York City. The CDC definition [to include women] definitely wouldn't have been changed. Also, ACT UP forced a focus on [treatments for] opportunistic infections [caused by AIDS], which kept people alive longer so that they were there when the good meds came [in 1996 and beyond].

Murphy: Would some of that have happened anyway?

Schulman: I don't know. I do know that people who were in ACT UP who have lived would've died, because they wouldn't have had access to the cutting-edge treatments. Also, ACT UP pushing parallel track [for drug trials] was crucially important, getting rid of restrictions like having to give up one drug to take another, trying to get rid of trials with a placebo [fake drug] arm was important. And of course one of the greatest treatment accomplishments that a faction within ACT UP almost stopped was proving the efficacy of AZT as a drug to prevent women from passing HIV to their babies.

Murphy: OK, final question. I know you did not write the copy on the back of the book, but it says that ACT UP "changed America forever." Do you agree?

Schulman: It changed me. It showed me that a movement can succeed.

Murphy: But do you think it changed America?

Schulman: As stigmatized as HIV still is, America has changed from a time when people were firebombing the homes of kids with hemophilia because they had AIDS, to where we are now—and how gay people are viewed now. And ACT UP changed the way that PWAs and gay people saw themselves, and it's changed our presence in the media. What's happened with that presence since is kind of pathetic. It's become very middlebrow. Which is why this is a story that still needs to be told accurately.

Choral History

Jay Vithalani / 2021

Originally published in *A&U*, August 6, 2021. Reprinted with permission of the author.

On a sweltering July day, I meet Sarah Schulman to talk about her new book, *Let the Record Show: A Political History of ACT UP New York, 1987–1993* (Farrar, Straus and Giroux). It is a large book, done on a large scale. It is not, however, an encyclopedia. Every part of the subtitle matters, from the indefinite article "a" to the terminal date "1993."

The primary material for Schulman's book is the ACT UP Oral History Project, a series of nearly two hundred interviews she and filmmaker Jim Hubbard conducted from 2001 to 2018 with surviving members of ACT UP. *Let the Record Show* is necessarily a choric work, layered with voices (including the author's). This quality makes the work difficult to capture in summaries, reviews, interviews—which perhaps explains why commentaries so far have concentrated largely on, and quoted almost exclusively from, the Preface and Introduction, a nonnarrative distillation in which Schulman outlines her intent, method, structure.

Schulman has the calmness and easy eloquence of someone who's been interviewed *many* times. (I apologize, twice, about potentially asking a few bog-standard questions for which—as the record shows—the response could simply be "Asked and answered!" She smiles and says, "I'm a professional," the first time, and "It is what it is" the second.) Along with this comes an Erin Brockovich–like capacity for recalling details about the dozens of people she writes about.

This is not at all to say that her tone is one of polite urbanity or that her conversation is passionless recitation. Moments of shaking-my-head exasperation, combative bewilderment, constantly shine through. Schulman is not given to self-deprecation, and she is unflinching when it comes to defending her historiographical practice.

Before we start the interview, I give her a copy of *A&U*'s August 2000 issue (Kevin Bacon is on the cover), in which she had been featured: an extract from her novel *The Child*, and an interview about writing lesbian fiction in the age of protease inhibitors. As she pockets the magazine she says wryly, "These photographs look familiar. I haven't made a lot of money in the last twenty years. I still live in the same rented sixth-floor walkup."

The following extracts have been edited for length and clarity.

Jay Vithalani: First things first—congratulations! *Let the Record Show* is your twentieth book. And it has received a great deal of attention and praise.

Sarah Schulman: Thank you!

JV: You've been writing about AIDS for a long time now, nearly forty years. How did that come about?

SS: I started working for a series of gay underground newspapers in the late seventies. These were gay and feminist papers that the mainstream ignored completely, and I was a girl reporter, twenty-three or twenty-four.

The identification of what we eventually called AIDS began in 1981. I started writing about AIDS because that is what was happening. I covered pediatric AIDS, women being excluded from experimental drug trials, homeless people with AIDS. By the time ACT UP was founded in March 1987, I had been writing about AIDS for about five years.

After I left ACT UP in mid-1992, I continued to write about AIDS. I wrote a book about gentrification, the relationship between AIDS and gentrification. I covered HIV criminalization. In 2001 Jim Hubbard and I started the ACT UP Oral History Project. So, I never stopped. I've spent my entire writing life writing about AIDS. But it's not the center issue for me, it's a side thing.

JV: Now, *that's* really interesting. You've never stopped writing about AIDS. *Let the Record Show* has been called—some quotes from the dustjacket—"a definitive and monumental history" (Michelangelo Signorile), "a masterpiece of historical research and intellectual analysis" (Alexander Chee), "epic, important, and moving" (Eve Ensler). And yet it's not a central preoccupation?

SS: A lot of things I say in *Let the Record Show* are things I've been saying for decades. It's about men, it gets a better publisher, it gets more attention, I get a higher level of access, and people now respond, "You're *so* smart!" Some of the ideas are not even *my* ideas, these are the ideas of a whole community.

JV: How does this relate to your cultural and political criticism, as well as your fiction?

SS: Because I'm a novelist, I know how to tell a story that works cumulatively, and a lot of nonfiction writers don't know how to do that. I'm able to build the information, and that's why it's readable. I have the skill to do something that's in a horizontal structure.

However, emotionally and artistically it's a lesser project, because I'm not looking into my soul to produce an idea. My job is to represent other people in a way that is accurate to who they are and what they say about themselves. There are a lot of people in the book I don't like, don't agree with. But I don't think you could tell which ones, because I think I was very fair. And that was my job. *Let the Record Show* is really not about me, and the other books are. I don't even remember writing this book.

JV: Wait—you don't remember writing this book? It sprang from your head like Minerva?

SS: One memory: I was at MacDowell and I remember looking at the printer. But I don't remember struggling. Because I had the original material and then I did a sort of mathematical cohering of what was in that material. I found the structure for it. But it's all about facilitating other people and so it's not as difficult in some ways.

JV: You give voice—many of the actual words in the book are not yours, they're words you've preserved—to a motley crew.

SS: It's a very special group of people. They're highly individuated. They disagree about a lot of things and tell the stories very differently. And *that's* the reality, that's the history. That's the part you can only show, you can't just say it. The reader has to experience that. You know how, when you take a creative writing class and they say, "Show, don't tell"? The reader really has to inhabit all the contradictions, as they're reading, to understand what the group relationship was like.

But ACT UP activists are also normal people. They are not "clean" people. And normal people can change the world, and that's very important to know. You don't have to be a saint. It's also very important to say when you were wrong. Very, very important. And people make mistakes all the time and people are wrong all the time.

JV: In the Introduction you say that one uniting feature of ACT UP members was characterological. Could you tell me a little bit about that?

SS: When Jim Hubbard and I started the Oral History Project, one of our big questions was "What do these people have in common?" At first we thought it was going to be experiential. If you analyze the questions over the years, they change. In the first three years I asked, "Did your family go to church?

Were they community oriented?" I was trying to find that kind of pattern. But it wasn't true and we had to drop it.

Then we thought maybe everybody had some foundational AIDS experience. And they didn't. People who didn't know anybody with AIDS came to ACT UP. After about seven years I finally realized it was a type of person, the kind of person who couldn't be a bystander, that it was characterological. It took a long time to figure that out.

JV: One way to read the book is as a counternarrative to David France's *How to Survive a Plague*. Much has been made of that.

SS: But it's not only that. It's part of a larger problem. For example, when I wrote an article for *T* magazine, the gay male editor changed "ACT UP" to "Larry Kramer's ACT UP." It's an American thing. Now we have the mythologizing of Anthony Fauci—there's always a white man who's going to save everybody. And David did that too, and other people do that. But nothing works that way, it's not accurate.

JV: Related to this, the reaction that there is a distortive recentering or overrepresentation in your account?

SS: I don't agree that I recenter, I think that's inaccurate. People say, "Oh, you've foregrounded women and people of color." I did not. I just said what they did. If you just say what people in ACT UP did, you get this very diverse, complex spread; and if you hide what they did and only show five people, it's not accurate. I don't think that I overrepresented anybody. Most of the people in my book are white men who've never been historicized before.

JV: Turning to accuracy and inaccuracy. Ben Ryan, in his review of the book in *The Guardian*, has said that you can be cavalier with facts. How do you respond to claims that you've made factual errors?

SS: Let me first say that I've had many book reviews, I've written twenty books, I've had hundreds and hundreds of reviews, and very few reviewers actually see the book the way I see it, whether it's praise or criticism. The most helpful review I've ever had was a critical review by Vivian Gornick of *Rat Bohemia*, where she said that these people are not bohemians, because bohemians choose to opt out of bourgeois life, and these people were thrown out. And I thought, "Wow, that's right." I learned a lot from that.

My book is an oral history. What oral history "proves" is that this is what people say about their experience. It doesn't even prove that this is really what they think about their experience. So, it's simply a record of what they say about it. It can seem nothing more than that, but when it's a critical mass—in this case I think there are 140 people I use in the text—you really start to see dimensions and shapes and patterns. And that's revealing, it's larger than anything one person says. You don't fact-check oral history. Because it's not fact. It's only the fact that the people who lived the history said that. Oral histories are not new, they're not controversial.

Ben was very odd. He called at least five people in ACT UP to claim that I did not do fact checking. Primarily, he seems to not understand what oral history is. Clearly, it reveals disagreements, contradictions and the fact that there is no single truth. Why he could not comprehend this is unclear to me.

JV: You wrote an opinion piece for *The Guardian* which received some pushback from two prominent gay British activists, which then got amplified on social media.

SS: That's crazy.

JV: All right, tell me why that's crazy.

SS: These men are saying that I was writing gay men out of AIDS history? That is not an accurate representation of what I'm doing. I think that it's some kind of kneejerk sexism. "You're going to take something away from us." I'm actually affirming them. They're just so sexist they can't just let it happen. Too bad for them. Hopefully, they'll read *the book* and they can send me an apology. The book is mostly about gay men.

JV: So the issue now is that of "erasure." Michael Specter in the *New Yorker* suggests there is an erasive vein in the book.

SS: Michael Specter is gatekeeping. I mean, it's sad. The *New York Times* allowed the book to be seen for what it is, *New York Magazine* allowed that. But the last bastion, where white straight men are in control, is the *New Yorker*. When David Remnick [editor of the *New Yorker*] interviewed me, he was all about Tony Kushner, Anthony Fauci, Larry Kramer. He didn't mention any of the 140 people who the book is about. The gatekeepers are so afraid they're going to lose the sense of themselves as objective and neutral. And heroes of the world. Specter says I'm wrong. It was a little group of five men who did everything. And actually, "No, *you're* wrong!"

JW: The title of the review in the *Times Literary Supplement*, "Kramer vs America," is a faux pas, I think.

SS: Regarding the *TLS*, as many people have pointed out, the reviewer [Omar G. Encarnación] clearly did not read the book, because the claims he makes in his opening paragraphs are refuted as early as the Introduction in *Let the Record Show*. It's hard for reviewers to complete a seven-hundred-page book, but when they agree to review it they are promising to do so.

JV: I'm going to shift gears a little bit. A TV series based on *Let the Record Show* is in the works, with Andrew Haigh as director and showrunner—exciting news! Tell us about that project?

SS: I was approached by Christine Vachon, a major player in world cinema, and a former member of ACT UP. Her partner, Marlene McCarty, was the only woman in Gran Fury [an artist collective of AIDS activists, 1988–1995]. The chance of having a woman producer who was in ACT UP means that the chances of the show being authentic are much higher. Christine brought in Jonathan King, who had done *When They See Us* on TV. He also did *Spotlight*. So here's someone who has a lot of experience bringing social justice stories to the screen at a very high level. The combination seemed perfect. Then we had to get a writer. We sent out the material to a lot of writers. And, really, everybody was afraid of it.

JV: Any names you can mention?

SS: No. But I would say probably about twenty writers. TV writers aren't political. This is also formally complex, it's not about five people on a journey, it's about a community. And unless you count *Game of Thrones*, there aren't many models for that. Andrew really wanted to do it. So I started looking at the history of his work. It's very classy. *Weekend* is a classic, and it's very relational. Andrew reveals social realities through intimate relationships. Then he turns around and does *45 Years*, with Charlotte Rampling, and gets an Oscar nomination. He also did the HBO series *Looking*. He has a very wide palette. So it seemed like a really good match. We'll see. He hasn't finished the pitch yet, so it hasn't been put up for sale yet. I don't have a sense of a timeline.

JV: When the manuscript was finished was there a bittersweet moment? Letting go?

SS: I don't think so, no. When a book of mine is printed I read it again, then I never read it again.

JW: That's very Elizabeth Bishop.

SS: Very Elizabeth Bishop?

JW: Yeah, that's what she said about her poems. Once she finished writing and revising and publishing them, they were finished objects, done.

SS: I hope I don't end up like Elizabeth Bishop, she had a terrible ending. She drank herself to death.

JW: I doubt that's what is going to happen to you. But what's next for Sarah Schulman?

SS: Oh, a lot. I have a new novel, a lesbian novel. I've finished a movie script about Carson McCullers. A young director has taken a shopping agreement on it and it's being packaged by her apparatus. I have a bunch of plays that I've been trying to get produced for years—still trying. I've also been working with Marianne Faithfull for the last number of years.

JW: It sounds like you're a workaholic.

SS: Really?

JW: Well, with so many projects going on at once, some finished, some simmering on the back burner, others being conceived right now.

SS: I don't think I'm a workaholic. I think that a lot of my work doesn't get to see the light of day. I have to fight for it for years and years and years. I also think that writing is very easy for me. So, in that sense I don't have to be a workaholic.

JW: But you are going on a much-deserved vacation soon, yes?

SS: Yes, to Hudson Valley and Provincetown with my girlfriend. Counting the days!

Index

A&U, 158
Abramović, Marina, 55
Academy Award (Oscar), 80
Acker, Kathy, 71, 86
ACT UP (AIDS Coalition to Unleash Power), 10, 14, 25, 32, 49, 60, 74, 79–81, 90, 97, 108, 109, 113, 117, 129, 157–58, 161–62; art and video work, 60, 150, 153; coalition and democratic structure, 54, 132–33, 151–52; conflicts within, 20–21, 113, 144, 155–56; constituents, 53–54, 61, 83, 116, 133, 151, 153–55, 159–60; in Germany, 115; Latino involvement, 150–52; legacy, 51–52, 132, 148; structure, 133–34; successes and failures, 54, 82, 133, 148–49, 151, 155–56; tactics and campaigns, 33, 53–54, 58, 108, 131–32, 134, 139, 148–50, 152–56
ACT UP Oral History Project, 46, 49, 58–60, 62, 72–73, 81, 84, 91, 105, 107, 109, 117, 129, 132–33, 139–40, 148, 150, 157–60
Advocate, The, 15, 27, 29
AIDS (acquired immunodeficiency syndrome), 18, 23–25, 27, 33, 45, 51, 53, 58, 60–61, 69, 84, 87, 107–8, 109, 133, 145, 149; activism, 5, 18–19, 23, 49, 72–73, 112, 116, 121, 133, 148, 150, 153–56, 162; and art production, 45; and bathhouse closings, 50, 80, 89, 115, 121; and Black men in the South, 145; and Christian paradigm of suffering, 37–38; drug use and needle exchange, 111, 133, 148, 150, 154, 156; and HIV criminalization, 88–89, 92, 94, 109–10, 158; and HIV prevention, 116; and HIV transmission, 109, 111–14; and HIV treatments and drug trials, 52–53, 115, 121, 131, 134, 148, 151, 154–56, 158; homelessness and housing, 24, 45, 50, 89, 121, 133, 148, 150, 156, 158; and homosexuality, 76; and media misrepresentation, 59–60, 72–73, 80–83, 112, 140, 150–51, 154, 160; and memorialization of 9/11, 73–75; and monogamy, 114; pediatric, 89, 115, 121, 158; and prison inmates, 133; and race, 145, 148; in the Soviet Union, 88, 115–16, 121; stigmatization and social neglect, 10, 13–14, 19, 23, 54, 80, 82, 131–32, 134, 139, 156; and women, 50, 53, 114, 116, 121, 150–51, 154–56, 158; writing about, 19–20, 90–91, 158
Akerman, Chantal, *Ma mère rit*, 84
Alameddine, Rabih, 62, 85–86; *I, the Divine*, 85; *Koolaids*, 85

165

INDEX

Albers, Patricia, *Joan Mitchell: Lady Painter*, 62
Alcoholics Anonymous (AA), 117, 119, 128
Allen, Woody, 7
Allison, Dorothy, 90; *Bastard Out of Carolina*, 76, 90
American Medical Association, 50
American Psychiatric Association, 50
American Repertory Theater, 46, 104
Antrim, Donald, 75
Arab Film Festival, 55
Arendt, Hannah, *The Origins of Totalitarianism*, 103
Aronson, Billy, 27
Arsenal Pulp Press, 70, 94, 125, 136
Astor Place, 108, 124
Audre Lorde Project, 48
Auster, Paul, 76
Avery, Ellis, 71
Avon Books, 76
AZT (azidothymidine), 25, 112–13, 131, 156

Bacon, Kevin, 158
Baker, Kevin, "The Death of a Once Great City," 129
Baldwin, James, *Another Country*, 63, 68, 94
Balzac, Honoré de, *Cousin Bette*, 45–46, 63, 68, 88, 94–95
Barnes, Djuna, 125
Barnes & Noble, 76, 90
Beacon Press, 69
Bechdel, Alison, 121
Beller, Tom, 75
Bellow, Saul, 55
Bishop, Elizabeth, 95, 162
Black LGBT Film Festival, 55
Black Lives Matter, 126
Black Panthers, 49
Bluestockings, 71
BOMB Magazine, 15
Bowles, Jane, 9

Boyd, Nan Alamilla, 86
Boys in the Band, The, 112
Brecht, Bertolt, 39; *The Threepenny Opera*, 107
Brim, Matt, 86, 145; *Poor Queer Studies*, 86
Bristol Myers Squibb (BMS), 151
Brockovich, Erin, 157
Brooklyn Museum, 55
Brown, Claude, *Manchild in the Promised Land*, 8
Brown, Margaret Wise, *Goodnight Moon*, 84
Brown, Michael, 137
Brown, Rita Mae, *Rubyfruit Jungle*, 20
Brown Foundation Fellowship, 62
Bumpers, Eleanor, 13
Burgess, Anthony, *A Clockwork Orange*, 63
Burton, Joseph, 26
Bush Doctrine, 45
Butler, Judith, 45

Califia, Pat, 90
Callen, Michael, 115
Callen-Lorde Community Health Center, 48
Carroll & Graf, 41, 69
Carrasco, Cesar, 105
Centers for Disease Control and Prevention (CDC), 151, 153, 156
Chee, Alexander, 158
City College of New York (CCNY), 140
Cleaver, Diane, 26
Clinton, Bill, 52
Clinton, Hillary, 96
Cohens, Hattie Mae, 13
Cole, Teju, *Open City*, 62
Colette, 64, 98–99; autobiography, 64
College of Staten Island CUNY, 58, 62, 66, 74, 84, 107, 109, 118, 126, 145
Columbia University, 146

Committee for Abortion Rights and Against Sterilization Abuse (CARASA), 88
Congress of Racial Equality (CORE), 49
Cooper, Amy, 136
Cooper, Anderson, 58
Cooper, Christian, 136
Cooper Union, 80
COVID-19 (Coronavirus disease), 132, 134, 154
Cowen, T. L., 102
Critical Legal Thinking, 132

Daley, Sandy, *Robert Having His Nipple Pierced*, 75
Dallas Buyers Club, 80
Daughters of Bilitis, 89
Dave, Naisargi, *Queer Activism in India*, 84
De Niro, Robert, 27
Delany, Samuel, 45
Democratic Party, 52–53, 73
DeSanti, Carole, 27
Dinkins, David, 154
Dolezal, Rachel, 155
Duke University Press, 23, 62, 68
Dunning, Jennifer, 92
Dutton, E. P., 6, 26–27, 90
Dyke March, 140
Dykes Against Racism Everywhere, 121

Eisenhower, Dwight D., 96
Empire State College SUNY, 88
Encarnación, Omar G., 161
Enemies, A Love Story (Mazursky), 37, 39
Ensler, Eve, 158
Essence, 145
Eugenides, Jeffrey, 75

Facebook, 60, 77, 96, 103, 120, 137, 155
Faithfull, Marianne, 129, 162
Farrar, Straus and Giroux, 140, 144, 150

Fauci, Anthony, 154–55, 160–61
Felix, Dia, *Nochita*, 84
Feminist Press, 117, 124
Firebrand Books, 4
Fitzgerald, F. Scott, 55
Fitzhugh, Louise, *Harriet the Spy*, 84, 98–99
Fox, The, 54
Ford Foundation, 73, 150
France, David: *How to Survive a Plague* (book), 112, 160; *How to Survive a Plague* (film), 82–83, 148
Frank, Anne, *The Diary of a Young Girl*, 36, 84, 98–99
Franke-Ruta, Garance, 83
Franzen, Jonathan, 55, 75
Freud, Sigmund, 98
Friedman, Kinky, 138
Fulbright Fellowship, 62, 109

Galás, Diamanda, 41–42, 69
Game of Thrones, 162
Gandhi, Mahatma, 49
Garner, Eric, 118, 137
Gay and Lesbian Alliance Against Defamation (GLAAD), 15, 53
Gay and Lesbian Victory Fund, 32
Gay Community News, 6, 88
Geffen, David, 27
Genet, Jean, *Funeral Rites*, 62, 85
Gilead Sciences, 112
Glee, 53
Goldstein, Richard, 89
Gonsalves, Gregg, 116
Goodreads, 142
Gornick, Vivian, 62, 77, 84, 160; *The Old Woman and the City*, 84
Gowdy, Trey, 122
Graeber, David, *Debt*, 136
Gran Fury, 162
Grand Central Station, 108
Grier, Barbara, 89

Griffin, Susan, 90
Guardian, The (New York), 88
Guardian, The (UK), 160–61
Guggenheim Fellowship, 62, 109
Gulf War, 108

Haifa Women's Center, 59
Haigh, Andrew, 161–62; *45 Years*, 162; *Looking*, 162; *Weekend*, 162
Hamlet, 95
Hammett, Dashiell, 119
Hanks, Tom, 83
Hansberry, Lorraine, 86
Harper's Magazine, 129, 146; "Letter on Justice and Open Debate," 146
Harrington, Mark, 151
Harris, Craig, 91
Harvard University, 73, 153
Hart, Ellen, 119
Hashimoto, Emily, 129
Haslip, Katrina, 152
Haynes, Todd, 139
Heller, Trude, 99
Helms, Jesse, 37, 139
Hemingway, Ernest, 55
Hemphill, Essex, 90–91
HERE (arts center), 36
Highsmith, Patricia, 99
Hilferty, Robert, 115
Hill, Marjorie, 154
HIV (human immunodeficiency virus). *See* AIDS
Hodes, Martha, 86
Home Box Office (HBO), 79, 162
hooks, bell, 103, 136; *All about Love*, 136
Howard, Jackson, 144
Hubbard, Jim, 46, 49, 56, 72, 82, 90–91, 102, 115–16, 129, 132, 139–40, 150, 157–59
Hudson, Rock, 151
Human Rights Campaign (HRC), 32, 53, 73

Hunter College, 47, 88, 98, 138
Hunter College High School, 87, 99
Hyde Amendment, 88

Irish Lesbian and Gay Organization, 108

James, Henry, 63
Jen, Gish, 76
Jenner, Caitlyn, 101
Jewish Voice for Peace, 84, 107
Jones, Tayari, 86

Kagan, Elena, 87, 99
Keene, John, *Counternarratives*, 85
Kennedy, John F., 96
Kerouac, Jack, 9, 18, 85; *Visions of Cody*, 85
Kessler Award, 45, 62
Key West Literary Seminar, 87
Kids Are All Right, The, 54
Killing of Sister George, The, 54
King, Charles, 154
King, Jonathan, 162; *Spotlight*, 162; *When They See Us*, 162
King, Martin Luther, Jr., 49–50; "Letter from Birmingham Jail," 50
Kingston, Maxine Hong, *Tripmaster Monkey*, 85
Kirkus Reviews, 6
Kitsch, Taylor, 81
Koch, Ed, 79, 88
Korie, Michael, 23–24, 26
Kramer, Larry, 79–82, 139, 151, 154–55, 160–61; *The Normal Heart*, 79–82
Kushner, Tony, 161; *Angels in America*, 81–82, 112–13

La Jolla Playhouse, 88, 95
LA Weekly, 41
Ladder, 89
Lambda Legal Defense and Education Fund, 32

Lambda Literary Awards, 19
Larson, Jonathan, 23–28, 122, 140; *Rent*, 23–28, 122, 140; *Superbia*, 27; *Tick, Tick... BOOM!*, 27
Law & Order, 100, 123
Lawlor, Andrea, *Paul Takes the Form of a Mortal Girl*, 129
Lee, Don L., 48
Leonard, Zoe, 134
Lesbian, Gay, Bisexual & Transgender Community Center, 79
Lesbian and Gay Studies and Queer Theory Conference, 59
Lesbian Avengers, 11, 21, 49, 109, 117, 140
Lesbian Herstory Archives, 102
Lesbian Poetry: An Anthology, 48
Let the Record Show..., 132
Levin, Jenifer, *Water Dancer*, 9
Levine, Debra, 133
Lewis, Robin Coste, *Voyage of the Sable Venus and Other Poems*, 84
Link, Derek, 155
Livingston, Jennie, 21, 154; *Paris Is Burning*, 21, 139
"Literature in the Age of AIDS," 87
Log Cabin Republicans, 73
Lorde, Audre, 15, 47–49, 65, 85, 88, 99, 102, 105, 108, 138; "The Transformation of Silence into Language and Action," 47, 85, 105, 108; *Zami*, 15
Los Angeles Review of Books, 87
Los Angeles Times, 120
Lucas, Craig, 37
Lyric Opera of Chicago, 25

MacDowell artist residency, 9, 70, 159
Madame Bovary, 98
Manzie, Sam, 40, 42
Marx, Karl, 98; *Communist Manifesto*, 105
Maso, Carole, *Ghost Dance*, 9

Massa, Robert, 89
Mattachine Society, 34–35
Maxwell, Roberta, 95
McCarthyism, 125–26
McCarty, Marlene, 162
McCullers, Carson, 36, 62, 84–85, 104, 162; *The Ballad of the Sad Café*, 85; *The Member of the Wedding*, 85
McCullers, Reeves, 104
McGovern, Terry, 151
McNamara, Robert, 108
McRae, Carmen, 99
Meaker, Marijane (Vin Packer), 99
Merrill, Jean, *The Pushcart War*, 84
merritt k, 142, 145
Middlebury College, 144
Millet, Kate, 104
MIX NYC Queer Experimental Film Festival, 49, 56, 60, 73, 75, 84, 90, 97, 107, 139
Mock, Brian, 13
Monk, Meredith, 67
Moody, Rick, 75–76
Moore, Carley, *The Not Wives*, 124
Morris, Tracie, 86
Morrison, Toni, 55
Moss, Jeremiah, *Vanishing New York*, 129
Museum of Fine Arts, Houston, 62
Museum of Modern Art (MoMA), 55–56
Myles, Eileen, *Inferno*, 75

Naiad Press, 4, 6, 89
Nana, 98
Nation, 31, 89
Narcotics Anonymous (NA), 117, 128
National Endowment for the Arts (NEA), 21
National LGBTQ Task Force, 73
National Organization for Women (NOW), 88
National Public Radio (NPR), 59, 65, 72, 95

170 INDEX

Navarro, Ray, 154
Naylor, Gloria, *The Women of Brewster Place*, 8
Nelson, Cary, 147
New American Library, 7
New Museum, 132
New York, 27
New York City Council, 80
New York City Hall, 50, 80, 88
New York Institute for the Humanities, 84, 107
New York Native, 80, 88–89, 115, 154
New York Police Department, 126
New York Press, 26
New York Theater Workshop, 27–28, 129
New York Times, 6, 15, 26, 32, 70–71, 90, 92, 110, 112, 120–21, 138–39, 144, 150, 161
New York Times Magazine, 145
News, 6
Nicaraguan Revolution, 49
Nixon, Cynthia, 99
NYC St. Patrick's Day Parade, 49, 108

Oberlin College, 153
Olander, William, 132
Olsen, Tillie, 70–71
Otter, Kathy, 133
Out, 15, 28
Outlines, 27
OutWrite conference, 37, 90

Paglia, Camille, 30
Paley, Grace, 66–67, 70, 138
Papp, Joseph, 95
Paulus, Diane, 104
Pelosi, Nancy, 132
PEN America, 107
PEN Ten, 107
Pence, Mike, 122
Penguin Books, 76
People Magazine, 8

PEP (postexposure prophylaxis), 113
Petit, Sarah, 28
Philadelphia, 83
Phillips, Caryl, 62
Picasso, Pablo, 121
Pickett, Billy Joe, 108
Playboy Enterprises, 26
Polgreen, Lydia, 145
Popham, Paul, 81
Port Authority Police Department, 118, 126
poststructuralism, 98
Povitz, Lana Dee, 143–44
POZ, 109
PrEP (preexposure prophylaxis), 112–13
Preston, John, 90–91
Princenthal, Nancy, *Agnes Martin: Her Life and Art*, 84
Proust, Marcel, 9
PS122 (art space), 36
Puar, Jasbir K., 114
Public Theater, 37, 79–80
Publishers Weekly, 6, 12, 74, 120–21
Puccini, Giacomo, *La bohème*, 24–25, 27–28
Pulitzer Prize, 80
Pyramid Club, 36

Queer|Art|Mentorship, 129
Queyras, Sina, 77
QW, 15

Radical Zappers of Feminist and Gay Liberation, 50
Rainer, Yvonne, 66
Rampling, Charlotte, 162
Rankine, Claudia, 62, 85–86, 136, 142, 145; *Citizen*, 85
Ratzinger, Joseph (Pope Benedict XVI), 132
Reagan, Ronald, 8, 49, 79, 82, 99–100, 115, 121–22

Remnick, David, 161
Republican Party, 12, 34, 37, 101, 121–22, 155
Rescue Press, 129
Rhys, Jean, *Wide Sargasso Sea*, 86
Rich, Adrienne, 8, 31, 45, 102, 105; "Compulsory Heterosexuality and Lesbian Existence," 8, 31, 105
Rikers Island, 126
Robinson, Marty, 113
Roe v. Wade, 32, 99, 129
Rossellini, Isabella, 67
Rotello, Gabriel, 31
Roth, Philip, 7, 55
Ruffalo, Mark, 79
Rukeyser, Muriel, 86
Russo, Vito, 80, 113
Rutgers University, 114
Ryan, Ben, 160–61
Ryan, Hugh, 87

Salaita, Steven, 93
Sanders, Bernie, 96, 147
Sappho, 98
Schulman, Sarah: on adaptation, 38–39; on advertising as enemy of women, 95; advice to aspiring writers, 65–66; and anti-Semitism, 93, 147; and approach to nonfiction, 91, 93–94, 102–5, 138, 159; arrests, 50, 88, 108, 153; and Beat culture, 89–90; on biological determinism, 31; and cancel culture, 146; and Catholicism, 30, 32, 58, 132; and censorship, 21, 37, 45, 70, 107–8, 146; and the closet, 3–4, 12–13, 58, 69–70, 89, 153; on conflict and abuse, 92–93, 97, 99–100, 109, 118, 126, 136–38, 141–47; and connection to fictional characters, 7–8, 70, 125–26; and critique of gay arts community, 21; on cultural gatekeepers, 45, 91, 123, 161; on cultural production versus political work, 10, 11–12, 14; on cultural regression, 41; defense of community-based culture, 16, 33, 43, 100; on dialectic between blame and responsibility, 124–29; on difference between art and entertainment, 64, 123; and direct action, 11, 49–51, 58–59, 88, 132, 134, 152; in downtown world of queer artists and leftists, 138–39; as East Village resident and icon, 7, 68, 97, 105, 109, 124, 149–50; on ex-gay movement, 30; on familial homophobia and rejection, 16, 40, 42, 44–45, 56–59, 76–77, 82, 87, 91, 111, 113, 117, 128–29, 138, 145; on fear of dominant culture, 18, 47, 56; on fiction and social change, 11–12; on fictional form, 63, 65, 104–5, 118–19, 122; and first awareness of lesbianism, 98–99; on first play, 36–37; on gay and popular culture, 4, 9, 20, 53–54, 70, 89; and gay marriage, 32–33, 51, 82, 113–14; and gay military service, 33, 51, 114; on gay oppression, 8, 42, 51–52, 101–2, 109, 112; on genre, 7, 45, 55, 104, 119; and gentrification, 7, 45, 73–74, 91–92, 94, 102, 117–18, 121–22, 124, 129, 143, 158; goal as writer, 8, 10, 77; and healthcare reform, 111–13, 155–56; on heterosexuality, 45; Holocaust background, 37, 97–98, 116, 138, 140–41; and homonationalism, 82, 109, 114; on homophobia as pleasure system, 111; hostility toward, 96; illness, 149–50;

on imperialism, 14; and Israeli/Palestinian conflict, 59, 92–94, 109–10, 120, 137; as journalist, 9, 17, 50, 80, 84, 87–89, 91, 107, 115, 121, 154; on lack of lesbian media, 15; and lesbian aesthetics, 4; on "lesbian boyhood," 18; on lesbian misrepresentation, 122–23; and lesbian writing, 9, 12–13, 17–18, 45, 52, 71, 90, 119, 158; on marginality, 12, 22, 49; as mentor, 70–71, 145; on MFA programs, 66, 70–71, 138; on the need to challenge comfort, 57; on the need to talk in person, 106, 110, 137; and New York City, 65, 67, 68, 94, 129, 141; on opposition to new ideas, 81; as optimist, 42, 45, 58–59, 142, 147; on oral history, 160–61; and the Palestinian queer movement, 49, 59, 62–63; on personal need for collaboration, 10; on plot in fiction, 9; and the police, 92, 99–100, 102–3, 110, 118, 126–27, 136–37, 142–43, 147; as postmodernist, 119; on the power of resistance, 13–14, 155; and practical application of ideals, 137, 143; and publishing, 4, 6–7, 11, 15, 52, 55, 69–70, 76, 90–91, 93, 119–21; on readers, 64, 77–78; on reviewers, 160; on the rewards of victimization, 14, 57, 104, 136–37; on scapegoating and social anxieties, 109–11; and self-revelation, 9; and sex outside relationships, 29–30; as social critic and public intellectual, 7, 20, 87, 95; as student, 87–88; and teaching, 47–48, 56, 58, 66–67, 118, 126, 135, 146; and trauma, 37–38; and trigger warnings, 137, 146; on the tyranny of positive images, 3–4, 8, 38, 123; as underrated writer, 120; and utopian ideals, 142, 147; on the Western canon, 39; on the whiteness of gay media, 15; on witness fiction, 90; on writing and early identity, 107; on writing habits and philosophy, 20, 64–67, 108, 163; on writing for the theatre, 37–38, 45, 55

Works By: *After Delores*, 3, 6–7, 26, 71, 75, 119–20, 138, 144; *The Burning Deck*, 88, 95; *Carson McCullers (Historically Inaccurate)*, 36, 84–85, 104; *The Child*, 36, 40–42, 62, 69–70, 104–5, 117, 158; *Conflict Is Not Abuse*, 87, 89, 92–94, 96, 97–98, 104–6, 109, 118, 120–21, 125–27, 131, 136–38, 141–47; *The Cosmopolitans*, 63, 68–69, 84, 87–88, 94–96, 117, 122, 125, 141; *Empathy*, 11–14, 16, 18–19, 36, 62–63, 104; *The Gentrification of the Mind*, 45, 68, 73–75, 91–92, 97, 101–2, 105, 117–18, 120–22, 129, 143, 158; *Girls, Visions and Everything*, 7, 18, 89–90, 119; *Israel/Palestine and the Queer International*, 62–63, 68, 97, 120; *The Lady Hamlet*, 46; *Let the Record Show*, 131–33, 148–56, 157–62; *Lonely Hunter*, 85, 162; *Maggie Terry*, 117–19, 124–29; *Manic Flight Reaction*, 36; *The Mere Future*, 63–64, 68–69, 75–76; *My American History*, 26, 50, 91, 117, 121–22; *People in Trouble*, 5, 18–19, 23–28, 36, 71, 90, 117, 122, 140; *Rat Bohemia*, 26, 62, 69, 71, 77, 122, 160; *Shimmer*, 29, 117, 120, 125–26;

The Sophie Horowitz Story, 6–7, 17–18, 89, 119; *Stagestruck*, 23, 29, 97, 117, 120, 140; *Ties That Bind*, 44–45, 56–57, 62, 76–77, 87, 91, 97, 111, 117, 120, 128, 141
Schumer, Chuck, 132
Schwartz, Delmore, 7
Scribner's, 89
Seal Press, 4, 89
Sesame Street, 27
Shepard, Benjamin, *From ACT UP to the WTO*, 72
Signorile, Michelangelo, 158
Simmons, Stephen, 40
Singer, Isaac Bashevis, *Enemies, A Love Story*, 36–39
Skype, 60
Slate, 88
Smith, Mark Lonnie, 95
Smith, Patti, *Just Kids*, 75
Smith College, 102
Snyder, Orin, 24
social media, 103–4, 161. See also Facebook; Twitter
Sontag, Susan, 58, 117, 120; *AIDS and Its Metaphors*, 58
Sotiris, Panagiotis, "Against Agamben: Is a Democratic Biopolitics Possible?," 132
Specter, Michael, 161
Spielberg, Steven, 27
St. Mark's Place, 124
St. Patrick's Cathedral, 33, 58, 133
St. Vincent's Hospital Manhattan, 74
Staley, Peter, 116, 153
Stonewall, 34–35, 101
Stryker, Susan, *Transgender History*, 86
Students for Justice in Palestine, 84, 107
Suggs, Donald, 101, 130
Sullivan, Andrew, 101, 112; *Love Undetectable*, 29

Sundance Film Festival, 56
Sundance Theatre Lab, 104

T magazine, 160
Tea Party movement, 122
Tel Aviv University, 59, 141
Thomson, Lynn M., 26, 28
Thrasher, Steven, 121
Till, Emmett, 13
Times Literary Supplement, 161
Torch Song Trilogy, 112
Treatment Action Group (TAG), 151, 155
Trump, Donald, 101, 103, 105, 109–10, 122, 125, 127, 155
Truvada (Emtricitabine/Tenofovir), 112–13, 116
Tumblr, 142
Twitter, 120, 139

Understanding the New Black Poetry, 48
United in Anger: A History of ACT UP, 60, 68, 72, 82, 115–16, 132–33, 134, 148–50
University of California Press, 45
University of Chicago, 87–88, 94, 98, 108, 138
University of Illinois Urbana-Champaign, 93
University of North Carolina at Asheville, 87, 91
University of Pennsylvania, 47
US Food and Drug Administration (FDA), 131, 139

Vachon, Christine, 162
Vaid, Urvashi, 73, 121, 150
Venora, Diane, 95
Veselka (restaurant), 138
Village Voice, 50, 71, 89, 154
Villarosa, Linda, 140, 144–45
Vineyard Theatre, 37
Visual AIDS, 82–83

Voices of the Rainbow, 48
Von Praunheim, Rosa, 115
Vulture, 79

Walker, Alice, 4, 13; *The Color Purple*, 4, 8, 13
Weatherman Brink's Robbery and Trial, 9, 17–18
Weber, Max, 98
Weise, Don, 69
Weiss, Bari, 147
Wentzy, James, 60, 140
Werner, Eddie, 40
Wesleyan University, 153
White, Edmund, 42, 45, 71, 85
Whitney Museum Study Program, 153
Wieder, Judy, 27

Wikipedia, 96
Williams, Dan Keith, 133
Wilma Theater, 36
Wings, Mary, 119
Wolfe, Maxine, 153
Womanews, 9, 17, 88–89
Women's Liberation Zap Action Brigade, 50, 88
Wood, Thelma, 125
World Trade Center, 74
Wright, Richard, 85

Yaddo artist residency, 75–76
Yale University, 81, 151, 153
YouTube, 82–83, 90

Zionism, 110, 137

About the Editor

Will Brantley is professor of English at Middle Tennessee State University. He is author of *Feminine Sense in Southern Memoir,* editor of *Conversations with Pauline Kael,* and coeditor (with Nancy McGuire Roche) of *Conversations with Edmund White,* all published by University Press of Mississippi.

Printed in the United States
by Baker & Taylor Publisher Services